# FUZZY EXPERT SYSTEM TOOLS

# FUZZY EXPERT SYSTEM TOOLS

**Moti Schneider**
*Florida Tech, USA,* and
*Tel-Aviv University, ISRAEL*

**Abraham Kandel**
*University of South Florida*
*USA*

**Gideon Langholz**
*Tel-Aviv University*
*ISRAEL*

**Gerard Chew**
*Florida Tech*
*USA*

JOHN WILEY & SONS

Chichester • New York • Brisbane • Toronto • Singapore

Copyright © 1996 by John Wiley & Sons Ltd.
Baffins Lane, Chichester,
West Sussex PO19 1UD, England

| *National* | 01243 779777 |
| *International* | (+44) 1243 779777 |

*Other Wiley Editorial Offices*

John Wiley & Sons, Inc., 605 Third Avenue,
New York, NY 10158-0012, USA

Jacaranda Wiley Ltd, 33 Park Road, Milton,
Queensland 4064, Australia

John Wiley & Sons (Canada) Ltd, 22 Worcester Road,
Rexdale, Ontario M9W 1L1, Canada

John Wiley & Sons (Asia) Pte Ltd, 2 Clementi Loop #02-01,
Jin Xing Distripark, Singapore 0512

*British Library Cataloguing in Publication Data*

A catalogue record for this book is available from the British Library

ISBN 0 471 95867 0

Produced from camera-ready copy supplied by the authors using Microsoft Word.

Printed and bound by Antony Rowe Ltd, Eastbourne

*In memory of*

*Professor Wyllis Bandler*

*Scholar, scientist, and friend*

# CONTENTS

# PREFACE

This book is intended for students, researchers, and practitioners involved in the study, research, and development of complex intelligent systems of an increasingly broad range. As researchers and practitioners continue their efforts to build such complex systems, it is realized that *uncertainty* is not only embedded in human knowledge but that allowing some degree of uncertainty in the description of a complex system is perhaps the most significant way of simplifying it.

There are several fundamentally different types of uncertainty. However, the sources of uncertainty can be divided into two main categories:

- uncertainties in the knowledge base; and

- uncertainties in the information (data) provided by the user and\or by external sensors.

The various approaches to dealing with uncertainty require the determination of numerical parameters for certainty factors, degrees of membership, thresholds of substantiation, etc. Areas in which uncertainty must be handled include the certainty with which a given rule is presumed to be applicable, the degree to which each antecedent of the rule is substantiated, and the degree to which each antecedent contributes to the substantiation of the rule.

The various types of uncertainty can be properly characterized and investigated within the framework of *Fuzzy Set Theory*. Fuzzy set theory was originally proposed by Lotfi Zadeh as a means for representing uncertainty and formalizing qualitative concepts that have no precise boundaries. For example, there are no meaningful landmark values representing the boundaries between *low* and *normal*, or *normal* and *high*. Rather, such linguistic terms are formalized by referring to fuzzy sets of numbers.

Fuzzy set theory, while based upon multivalued logic, extends this logic in the same way that ordinary set theory extends binary logic. In particular, fuzzy set theory frees us from the law of contradiction and allows us to entertain conflicting propositions.

Thus, the ability to operate in *uncertain* or *unknown* environments is an essential component of any intelligent system and is particularly crucial to its performance. It reflects the fact that many applications involve human expertise and knowledge which are invariably imprecise, incomplete, or not totally reliable. Therefore, the intelligent system must combine knowledge-based techniques for gathering and processing information with methods of approximate reasoning. These would enable the system to better emulate human decision-making processes and to allow for imprecise information and/or uncertain environments.

Since uncertainty management is such an important characteristic of intelligent systems, *fuzzy inferencing* procedures are becoming, therefore, increasingly crucial to the process of managing uncertainty. Fuzzy set theory provides a systematic framework for dealing with fuzzy quantifiers and makes it possible to deal with different types of uncertainty within a single conceptual framework.

This book is concerned therefore with the representation and manipulation of fuzzy knowledge. It evolves around FEST (*Fuzzy Expert System Tools*), an *expert system shell* developed to incorporate the fuzzy parameters needed by the fuzzy rule-based system and to allow for fuzziness in both data and knowledge descriptions, whose key features include:

- handling fuzzy knowledge and data,
- the ability to reach multiple conclusions,
- order-independent inferencing,
- user-defined keywords and (their) synonyms,
- forward and backward chaining,
- natural language programming and interfacing,
- user-defined membership functions,
- explanation capabilities,
- processing clauses such as executable procedures, regular sentences, and mathematical expressions,
- extensive capabilities for file editing and maintenance.

The book consists of 11 chapters that deal with the various issues involved in representing and manipulating fuzzy knowledge. These issues include:

- introduction to fuzzy set theory,

- discussion of possibility-probability relation and of possibility measures,

- the processes of knowledge acquisition, knowledge representation (e.g., semantic nets, frames, and production rules), and knowledge generation,

- the notions of vagueness and fuzziness,

- issues involved in knowledge processing such as compiling subjective knowledge, processing clauses (e.g. executable procedures, regular sentences, and mathematical expressions), and creating the R-list,

- knowledge preprocessing in FEST,

- issues pertaining to inferencing procedures, fuzzy inferencing procedures, and inferencing procedures in FEST.

The authors gratefully acknowledge the contribution of Lauri Faussett and Susan Leonard to this book. The authors are particularly grateful to Peter Mitchell of John Wiley & Sons Ltd. for his help, encouragement, and patience. Moti Schneider would like to thank Marsha, Oren, and Leor for their support and encouragement. Abe Kandel would like to thank Nurit, Sharon, Gil, and Adi for their support and encouragement.

*Moti Schneider*
*Abe Kandel*
*Gideon Langholz*
*Gerard Chew*

*Florida, 1996*

# 1 INTRODUCTION

To understand various phenomena in the world around us, scientists often resort to mathematical modeling. In many cases, however, it is easier said than done. Sometimes, the phenomenon is so complex that it defies modeling, or that building a mathematical model is either an impossible task or unattractive. Scientists then try to relax the model by using heuristics to reason about the missing information in the model and about the phenomenon that this model represents. In other cases, we do not completely understand the phenomenon and must be satisfied with an incomplete model with which we can reason.

It turns out that many mathematical models do not emulate precisely the phenomena around us. Scientists, therefore, turn to building models that describe the phenomenon only partially and then reason about the rest. They use *artificial intelligence* (AI) to provide tools for reasoning and use them to understand complex or incomplete phenomena.

Artificial intelligence research in the past decade enjoyed many important successes. Possibly the most significant success has been the development of very powerful AI tools better known as *expert systems*.

## 1.1 Expert Systems

Expert systems have been defined in various ways, but all the definitions share a common thread suggesting that expert systems are artificial means used to emulate the way in which domain experts solve problems.

Edward Feigenbaum [3], one of the best known AI researchers, defined an expert system as follows:

> "An expert system is an intelligent computer program that uses knowledge and inference procedures to solve problems that are difficult enough to require significant human expertise for their solutions. Knowledge necessary to perform at such level, plus the inference procedures used, can be thought of as a model of the expertise of the best practitioners in the field.
>
> The knowledge of an expert system consists of facts and heuristics. The facts constitute a body of information that is widely shared, publicly available, and generally agreed upon by the experts in the field. Heuristics are mostly private, little-discussed rules of good judgment (rules of plausible reasoning, rules of good guessing) that characterize expert-level decision making in the field. The performance level of the expert system is primarily a function of the size and the quality of the knowledge base it possesses."

This definition, however, raises two questions. First, what is meant by problems that are difficult enough? If one has difficulties in spelling English words, will a computer spell-checker become an expert system? Or, if one has problems with arithmetic operations, will a calculator be considered an expert system? Our intuition tells us that neither speller-checkers nor calculators are expert systems since an expert system emulates experts and experts are not only task performers.

The second question relates to the definition of an expert. Who is an expert? Is an expert someone with an advanced degree in a certain specialty? How much does one have to know in order to become an expert? We know of many cases where people have no formal education, yet they can solve problems at least as good as "formal" experts. We also know of many cases where experts are divided in their opinion as to which is the proper or best approach to the solution of the problem (for example, in politics, economics, or medicine).

These questions suggest that it might be advantageous to characterize an expert system rather than attempt to define it. However, prior to doing so, note that the general idea of an expert system is to take advantage of the large memory capacity and speed of the computer, which can process large amounts of information at a fraction of the time that a human would require. The expert system incorporates the reasoning of human experts in a particular domain and combines it with the computer's processing speed and large memory capacity.

Let us now return to the five most important characteristics of an expert system:

1. *An expert system should be user-friendly.* Since the user is not necessarily familiar with the inner operations of the expert system, the expert system should be easy to use and its functionality should be self-explanatory. To accomplish this, the expert system should provide the user with help pages, use simple instructions to interface with the user, and should be menu-driven. In addition, the user should be able to maintain the knowledge and/or data bases, print parts of the knowledge and/or data bases, etc.

2. *An expert system should be able to learn from its past experience.* As with human experts, the ability to learn means that the expert system is able to reach similar solutions faster when the same problem is presented more than once. Basically, there are three types of learning associated with expert systems.

   (a) *Learning from examples.* The expert system generates knowledge regarding some problem domain when examples and test cases are provided. Its decision-making process is based on extrapolating the newly generated knowledge.

   (b) *Learning by analogy.* The expert system draws analogies between the problem at hand and its current knowledge derived from solving similar cases. When similar cases are detected, the expert system extracts their solutions and applies them to the new problem.

   (c) *Learning by skill refinement.* The expert system accepts new knowledge from the domain expert and incorporates it within the existing knowledge base. The expert system should be capable of validating the new knowledge against the existing knowledge and of ensuring that the knowledge is complete and not contradictory.

3. *Ability to explain.* Similarly to human experts, the expert system should be able to explain its reasoning process and answer questions about the inference procedures. The ability to explain is a very important feature of the expert system since it is the only way to make the user comfortable and confident that the decision-making mechanism of the expert system is at least complementary if not superior to his/her own decision-making process. The user can relate to the inference process and verify that the expert system does what it is supposed to do.

   Furthermore, the ability to explain is also important to the expert system designer and to the knowledge engineer. The expert system designer can use sample knowledge bases to validate the expert system, whereas the knowledge engineer can check whether the knowledge is complete and validated properly.

4.    *Approximate reasoning.* The expert system controls its actions until the final conclusion is reached. It keeps track of all the successfully completed tasks or sub-tasks and, if any information is missing, the expert system should pause and extract it from the user before proceeding. In any case, the expert system should always be able to decide the next step to take in the problem-solving process in order to avoid deadlock conditions.

Often, the data and knowledge about the problem domain are fuzzy or incomplete. Similarly to human experts, the expert system should also perform in uncertain environments by utilizing some kind of an intelligent guessing mechanism referred to as *uncertainty management* [45, 71, 116, 121].

5.    *Time constraint.* Often, the expert system is required to perform under time constraints. Many "real world" applications require *real-time* response. This means that the expert system must perform its tasks fast in order to be embedded in a "real world" application. In some cases this will mean finding "a good" solution to the problem and not necessarily the optimal one.

To implement some of the above characteristics, the expert system would generally consist of the nine components shown in Figure 1.1 and listed below.

1.    *User interface.* As was mentioned above, any expert system should provide an easy and friendly interface to the user. It should query the user in the simplest possible fashion and if necessary it should provide help pages.

2.    *Knowledge base.* The knowledge base contains all the relevant expertise necessary to solve a problem in a given domain. The knowledge base consists of heuristic rules as well as established facts and theories [81]. In most cases, the knowledge base is permanent and is rarely modified.

3.    *Data base.* The data base contains information specific to the problem domain, as well as information pertaining to reserved words and key words which are used by the inference engine in the inference procedure.

4.    *Inference engine.* The inference engine uses rules to infer appropriate conclusions based on relevant portions of the knowledge base. Similarly to human experts, the expert system should be able to arrive at the same conclusions independently of the order in which the relevant rules are fired. The inference mechanism should be flexible enough to justify the expectation of human-like reasoning [99, 101].

5.    *Blackboard.* The blackboard is a data structure that contains the initial data provided by some external devices or user input, as well as the intermediate result from the inference process.

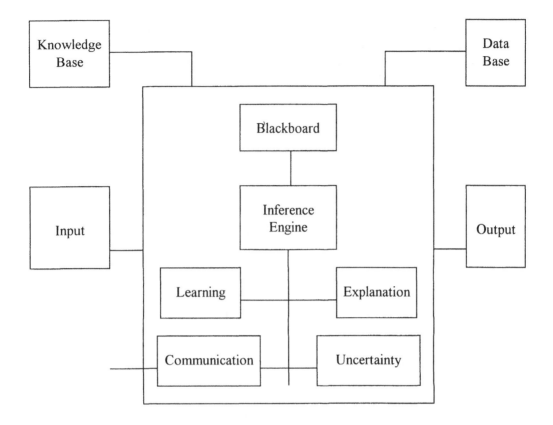

**Figure 1.1** General structure of an expert system

6. *Explanation program.* The explanation program explains the inference process and indicates how particular conclusions or actions were established.

7. *Learning program.* The learning program is activated after each execution by the inference engine. It analyzes the inference process, and establishes rules to speed-up the process for when the inference process will be activated again. The learning program is also responsible for establishing new confidence factors in various rules as the expert system matures.

8. *Communication to other expert systems.* Similarly to human experts, the expert system should be able to consult other expert systems when it encounters difficulties. Cooperating expert systems can add new dimensions to the decision-making process.

9.  *Uncertainty management program.* Uncertainty management is an imperative function of the expert system since the data and knowledge provided by the user are fuzzy, incomplete, or vague. Nevertheless, regardless of the vagueness of the data and knowledge, we still want the expert system to be able to infer under these conditions and solve problems using approximate reasoning [33].

## 1.2  Why Use Expert Systems?

It is quite difficult to represent human expertise in a computerized system. Even the successful expert systems, which were designed to perform like human experts, still provide only a small extension of expert's problem solving ability. Expert systems have no real intelligence and are often used only to supplement the expert as an advising or consulting tool.

So the question "Why use expert systems if we have human experts?" is a pertinent one. It turns out that there are several good reasons for using expert systems. To begin with, *artificial expertise is permanent*, like any other software. The data and knowledge are stored in computer memory and remain there unless we remove or change them. In contrast, human expertise is perishable. If we do not use certain data or knowledge often, we tend to forget.

*Artificial expertise produces consistent results.* Computers are not influenced by outside pressures and produce consistent results regardless of the complexity of the problem. Human expertise, on the other hand, is not always consistent. Human experts get tired or bored, the level of their performance may change if they are under pressure, and they may not produce the best results if the problem is very complicated or if it has to be solved quickly.

*Artificial expertise is affordable.* It takes about one year to develop an expert system compatible with a human expert, but it takes many years to "produce" a human expert. Human experts are relatively few whereas artificial experts are easily reproducible, can be distributed on disks, and are accessible to many.

*Artificial experts preserve knowledge.* Human experts change jobs, retire, or die and finding replacements of same quality and expertise is often impossible. On the other hand, once the human expertise has been captured within an expert system it is there to stay.

Of course, all of these beg the question "Will expert systems replace human experts?" The answer is definitely no. Human experts will always outperform artificial experts. Human experts are more creative than artificial experts and the scope of their knowledge is much broader. An artificial expert is restricted to a specific domain and no matter how sophisticated the expert system is, it can cover only a limited subset of the knowledge of the human expert. Moreover, the human expert can improvise and adapt if the problem is not precisely in his/her domain. In addition, the human expert can apply commonsense knowledge whereas the artificial expert utilizes technical knowledge which is very specific and has a very narrow focus.

Expert systems are constructed to mimic the reasoning process of human experts, to capture and preserve their knowledge, and to make this knowledge more accessible. Expert systems are sophisticated programs that utilize powerful computer resources to assist human experts in performing their tasks. Unlike human experts, expert systems do not learn from experience, they are incapable of making intelligent guesses or applying commonsense, and they cannot use rules of thumb in their decision-making procedures.

## 1.3 Historical Overview

We can distinguish three periods in the development of expert systems.

- **1960 - 1969.** During this period, expert systems were primarily developed in *scientific* domains. One of the first applications of expert systems in chemistry was *DENDRAL* [22], designed to interpret data from mass spectrometers and determine the structure of molecules. A speech-understanding expert system *HEARSAY* [20], along with a mathematical problem-solver *MACSYMA*, were also developed in this period [60].

- **1970 - 1979.** The early seventies were marked by the development of several expert systems in the field of *medicine*. *MYCIN* [88] was designed to help physicians diagnose meningitis and blood infections. *CASNET* and *INTERNIST* [60] were also designed in this period.

    Toward the end of the seventies, *PROSPECTOR* [18] was designed to predict potential *mineral deposits*. The first expert system whose subject domain was *education* was developed. Called *SOPHIE* [60], it taught electronic circuit troubleshooting.

- **1980 - present.** The early eighties brought popularity and commercial interest to expert systems following the success of expert systems designed in the previous period. This period is characterized by the *commercialization* of expert system development tools known as *expert system shells* (ESs).

    Expert systems of the first and second periods were hand-crafted, i.e. all the software components, as well as the knowledge base, were coded by their developers. The development of these expert systems involved a lot of human and computer resources. In their effort to reduce development costs, researchers came up with the idea of ESSs. An expert system shell is just a skeleton of an expert system with all the components of an expert system except the knowledge of a given area of expertise.

    For example, the *EMYCIN* (Essential *MYCIN*) [60] expert system shell is the *MYCIN* expert system without its knowledge. The *EMYCIN* was successfully used in the development of the *PUFF* [60] expert system which provides diagnostic consultations in the domain of pulmonary function disease. It was developed simply by populating the empty *EMYCIN* knowledge base with expertise in pulmonary function disease and using expert system functions available from *EMYCIN*.

Some of the domains of expert system applications include the following [56, 81].

- *Interpretation* - These expert systems infer situation descriptions from sensor data. Given a set of data, these expert systems attempt to make an intelligent decision of what the data mean. For example, the *DENDRAL* expert system has achieved a high level of performance by doing mass spectral analysis and determining the structure of molecules [22].

- *Planning* - These expert systems develop schema to achieve specified goals, policies, or plans. The *VIPS* (visual interactive planning system) is a very good example of an expert system used in planning. It uses *Petri nets* as a graphical language to specify goals [60].

- *Prediction* - These expert systems attempt to infer likely consequences of given situations. The *PROSPECTOR* [18] expert system predicts molybdenum mineral deposits, valued at over 100 million dollars, after analysis of geological data.

- *Consultation* - These expert systems provide consultative advice to human experts. *MYCIN* [88] was one of the first successful expert systems used for diagnosing and therapy recommendations for infectious diseases.

- *Diagnosis* - These expert systems attempt to infer system malfunctions from observations. *JET X* [87] is a PC-based expert system designed to diagnose faults in military aircraft engines.

- *Design* - These expert systems attempt to configure objects under constraints and design actions as applied to planning. Such systems aid designers and planners by providing them with the necessary expertise to help them make intelligent decisions. *ASDEP* is an expert system for power plant design [60].

- *Debugging* - These expert systems prescribe remedies for malfunctions and execute plans to administer the prescribed remedies. *AITEST* [5] is an expert system designed for debugging faulty modules, ports, junctions, etc.

- *Monitoring* - *PERF-EXS* is an example of a powerful monitoring expert system designed to be the plant operator helper. It monitors the performance of the entire plant and tries to detect deviations in the expected values of the various processes and diagnose the causes of malfunctions [60].

- *Training* - Training expert systems increases the skill level of the user in some particular subject domain. Usually the first step is to identify the knowledge level of the user in order to determine the goal (what should the user be taught). *SOPHIE* and *STEAMER* are examples of training expert systems [60].

- *Assisting* - These expert systems have expertise in a particular subject domain and are used to assist non-experts in their decision-making process. The decision-making capabilities of these expert systems are usually above or at the same level as a human expert. The *EXPLAIN* expert system was developed to assist non-experts in using a package of image processing algorithms [95].

## 1.4 Overview Of FEST

This book is about *FEST* which stands for *fuzzy expert system tools*. *FEST* is an expert systems shell that utilizes various newly-developed techniques in the area of expert systems.

The background material necessary for understanding the making of *FEST*, as well as the details of its various features, will be discussed in the following chapters. In this section, however, we summarize the basic attributes of *FEST*.

- *Fuzzy sets and fuzzy logic. FEST* uses fuzzy sets and fuzzy logic to overcome some of the problems which occur when the data provided by the user are vague or incomplete. However, there is nothing "fuzzy" about fuzzy sets and fuzzy logic. Fuzzy sets and fuzzy logic incorporate precise techniques for solving problems in which the information about the problem domain is fuzzy or incomplete.

- *Multiple conclusions.* One of the major differences between *FEST* and other expert system shells is that *FEST* can infer multiple conclusions. This is an important feature from the application point of view. *FEST* provides all possible solutions whose truth is above a certain threshold, and the user or the application program can then choose the appropriate solution depending on the particular situation.

- *Order-independent inferencing.* This feature is important for building a knowledge base. The fact that the user does not have to build the knowledge base in a certain order adds flexibility to the expert system and makes it more powerful. When the user enters new knowledge, it is simply appended to the end of the knowledge base. *FEST* arrives at the same conclusions regardless of the order in which the rules are stored in the knowledge base.

- *Keywords and synonyms. FEST* allows the user to define keywords and their synonyms. This feature brings *FEST* closer to the goal of being able to use natural language. By associating the words $\alpha$ and $\beta$ with the same meaning, the user may use them anywhere in the knowledge base because *FEST* searches for keywords and their synonyms during the inference process. For example, if $\alpha$ = "people" and $\beta$ = "persons", the user can use either one of these words to describe humans and does not have to remember to use only the word "people" in a context where "persons" is more suitable. Thus, this feature allows more flexibility in creating the knowledge base, and makes the expert system shell more user-friendly.

- *Forward and backward chaining.* The inferencing technique in *FEST* utilizes direct chaining which is based on the *forward chaining* inference procedure. This means that *FEST* searches for data that match the premise of a rule, and if it finds a match, it fires the conclusion. The explanation process in *FEST* is accomplished via *backward chaining*, namely, *FEST* tries to discover why a conclusion was fired.

- *Natural-language programming and interfacing.* *FEST* is mostly menu-driven. However, if the user has to provide *FEST* with certain information, he/she can do it in a natural language fashion. *FEST* parses the sentence, validates that it is grammatically correct, and then processes it.

- *Ability to explain its inferences.* When a conclusion is reached, the user can ask *FEST* to present its reasoning path. In addition, this feature allows the user to test the correctness of the knowledge base as well as to examine the reasoning path if the user does not remember all the combinations that lead to the firing of the conclusions. In any case, the user may check the validity of the knowledge base and modify it in cases where the conclusion reached is the wrong one.

- *Can be executed as subprogram from applications.* Expert system shells are not expert systems because they lack knowledge of the problems they are intended to solve. In other words, expert systems are designed to use expert system shells as a means to perform inferencing on a specific problem in a specific domain. The application program utilizes the expert system shell and uses its conclusions for further evaluations. For example, consider a communications expert system in which the application program provides the expert system shell with all the data from the data base. The expert system shell infers the best communication path, and then the result is sent back to the application program which establishes a communication link between the stations.

- *File editing and maintenance.* In addition to the usual editor functions, the most important feature of the editor in *FEST* is that of checking the validity of modified or newly entered rules. Whenever the user modifies the knowledge base, the editor checks the modified (or new) rules for their consistency with the grammar defined by *FEST*. For example, if the user forgets to add keywords such as *If* or *Then*, the editor will reject the rule.

- *Membership function generator*. *FEST* allows the user to define the membership functions that will be used in the inference process. This feature reduces the size of the knowledge base and, therefore, decreases the execution time of the inference engine. To illustrate this, consider the relationship between *age* and *weight*. In a conventional expert system, the user has to define *n* rules to describe this relationship, such as:

$$\textit{If } x \textit{ is } y_1 \textit{ years old Then } x \textit{ weighs } z_1 \textit{ kilograms}$$
$$\textit{If } x \textit{ is } y_2 \textit{ years old Then } x \textit{ weighs } z_2 \textit{ kilograms}$$

.
.
.

$$\textit{If } x \textit{ is } y_n \textit{ years old Then } x \textit{ weighs } z_n \textit{ kilograms}$$

In *FEST* on the other hand, we use membership functions to reduce the *n* rules into a single rule, called the *fuzzy If-Then rule*:

$$\textit{If } x \textit{ is OLD Then } x \textit{ is FAT}$$

where OLD and FAT are fuzzy sets.

## 1.5 About The Book

The book is divided into three major parts. The first part serves as an introduction. The current Chapter 1 introduces expert systems and discusses their major characteristics and their role in the design of intelligent systems. The installation procedure of *FEST* and some aspects of its operation are introduced in Chapter 2. We consider the major components of *FEST* and its main menus. Chapter 3 provides a brief introduction to fuzzy logic and Chapter 4 discusses some issues related to the theory of possibility.

The second part of the book deals with knowledge. The concept of knowledge is introduced in Chapter 5 where we explain the meaning of knowledge, its sources, and the various techniques used to represent it. In Chapter 6 we discuss the concept of vagueness in expert systems, and in Chapter 7 we show how to handle vagueness. In particular, we show how to parse and store vague (fuzzy) information, how to process it, and how to create links among pieces of knowledge that contain this kind of information. In Chapter 8 we discuss how this is done in *FEST*. In particular, we consider the concept of a fuzzy rule, and show how it is processed, manipulated, and how it is linked to other fuzzy rules via membership functions.

The third part of the book is devoted to the inference process. In Chapter 9 we discuss the three major inferencing methods which include forward chaining, backward chaining, and direct chaining. In Chapter 10 we explain how the inference procedure is implemented using direct chaining when the data and/or the knowledge are fuzzy, and in Chapter 11 we show how the direct chaining inference procedure is used in *FEST*. We explain the process of entering data and the inferencing process, and show how to use the explanation module and how to observe the inference chain.

*FEST* serves in this book as an example of a fuzzy expert system. The diskette provided with the book can be used to practice the introduced methods and to realize the power of fuzzy logic when it is combined with expert system technology to produce an intelligent tool called the *fuzzy expert system*.

# 2 GETTING STARTED

Using *FEST* requires only limited computer experience. We have achieved this by designing *FEST*'s user interface around a uniform menu system that considerably simplifies the task of working with the expert system tool.

This chapter provides an introduction to *FEST*'s user interface. It is concerned with the installation and execution of *FEST*, the use of menus, editing and browsing, and command line entries. The details of the inner working of *FEST*, which are transparent to the user at this level, are deferred to subsequent chapters.

## 2.1 Installation And Execution

To use *FEST*, you should have the following:

- IBM PC or true compatible with a 386 (or better) processor.

- PC-DOS or MS-DOS operating system, Version 5.0 or later.

- High density floppy-disk drive.

- Hard-disk drive with at least 2 MB free.

- Minimum 1 MB RAM internal memory. While this would suffice to run *FEST*, the execution speed will improve dramatically if you have 2 - 4 MB RAM set up as XMS or EMS memory.

The *FEST* distribution diskette contains an installation program. Place the distribution diskette in drive A or drive B, change your current drive to either A or B, and type INSTALL at the DOS prompt. The installation program will create a directory called FEST on your hard disk (C) and will install *FEST* in that directory.

Note that the installation program also creates a subdirectory called SYSTEM one level below the installation directory. All of *FEST*'s system files are placed in this subdirectory, and *FEST* looks there for all the required files. In addition, the installation program also creates a subdirectory called EXAMPLES one level below the installation directory. It is strongly recommended that you do not use the SYSTEM subdirectory for your own files, but rather use the EXAMPLES subdirectory to store your files.

To execute *FEST*, change to the drive and directory where *FEST* is installed, type *FEST* at the DOS prompt (note that the default directory C:\\*FEST* is assumed here and throughout this chapter), and press the **ENTER** key:

$$C:\backslash FEST > FEST \ [\textbf{ENTER}]$$

Note, however, that in many cases you may want to integrate or incorporate the fuzzy expert system tool within other environments. For example, you may write your own expert system and utilize *FEST* as an existing tool. In such cases, *FEST* can be invoked along with the following parameters: *KB (knowledge base)*, *DATA (data file)*, and *OUTFILE (output file)*. Let us briefly explain the meaning of these parameters.

When you type *FEST KB* at the DOS prompt,

$$C:\backslash FEST > FEST \ KB \ [\textbf{ENTER}]$$

you instruct *FEST* to load some knowledge base. This saves processing time if *FEST* is called from an application program. When this command is executed, the specified knowledge base is loaded, and the control is shifted to *FEST*. At this point, the main menu of *FEST* is displayed and you gain access to *FEST*. Note that here and in the remaining two cases, the file name of the knowledge base assumes the extension ".rul" unless you have already entered it.

When you type *FEST KB DATA* at the DOS prompt,

$$C:\backslash FEST > FEST \ KB \ DATA \ [\textbf{ENTER}]$$

the application program loads the specified knowledge base, as well as the data file which is loaded onto the blackboard. Again, after loading the two files, control is shifted to *FEST* and the main menu of *FEST* is displayed.

Finally, if you type *FEST KB DATA OUTFILE* at the DOS prompt,

$$C:\backslash FEST > FEST \ KB \ DATA \ OUTFILE \ [\textbf{ENTER}]$$

then upon reading these parameters, *FEST* changes its status to a non-interactive mode. This means that *FEST* loads the designated knowledge base and data file into its internal data structure, performs the inference procedure, and then writes the result(s) of the inference to the file specified by *OUTFILE*. These are all done while the control remains with the application program.

Note that if more than three parameters are provided to *FEST*, an error message is produced and *FEST* will not execute.

## 2.2 The Main Menu

Once the files have been properly installed and the *FEST* command has been invoked at the DOS prompt, the system is up and running. You are then presented with the main menu shown in Figure 2.1, which consists of four options:

- *File*
- *Grammar*
- *ES-Shell*
- *Quit*

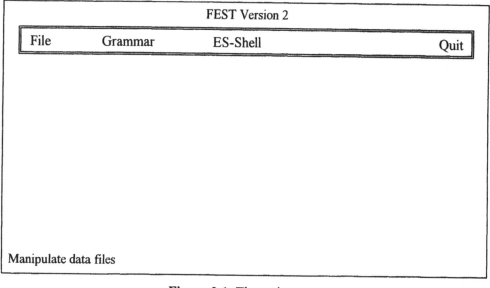

**Figure 2.1** The main menu

In the main menu and in any other *FEST* menu, you can choose any option using the arrow keys ($\uparrow$ and $\downarrow$ if the menu is vertical, or $\leftarrow$ and $\rightarrow$ if the menu is horizontal), the mouse (by moving the mouse cursor to the proper place in the menu), or by pressing the *highlighted* letter in any given option. To confirm your selection, press the **ENTER** key or the mouse left-button. The **ESC** key (or the right-button of the mouse) removes the current menu from the screen and shifts control to the previous option in the previous menu.

Note that some menu options are highlighted whereas other menu options are not. If a menu option is *not* highlighted, it means that this option is inaccessible temporarily. It serves to signal that some action is required *prior* to activating this menu option. For example, if a knowledge base has not been loaded yet, the menu options *Grammar* and *ES-Shell* are highlighted (inaccessible), implying that, prior to using these menu options, you must first load a knowledge base.

Let us now consider the four main menu items depicted in Figure 2.1. Here, we are concerned only with the main menu and the sub-menus that are one level below the main menu items, and defer the discussion of lower-level sub-menus to Chapters 8 and 11.

The selection of *File* from the main menu allows you to invoke programs for manipulating knowledge bases and synonym lists, for creating membership functions, and to exit temporarily to DOS. The *File* sub-menu is shown in Figure 2.2.

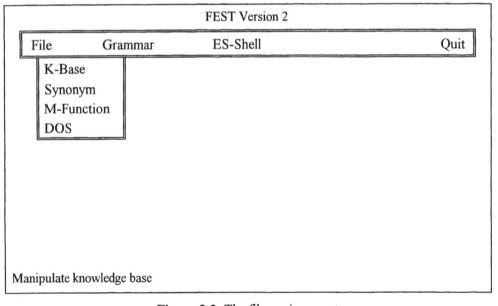

**Figure 2.2** The file environment

As seen in Figure 2.2, the *File* sub-menu shown consists of the following items.

- *K-Base*: This option allows you to manipulate a particular knowledge base.

- *Synonym:* This option is used to manipulate the synonym file.

- *M-Function:* This option invokes the program used to create membership functions.

- *DOS:* Selecting this option allows you to exit *FEST* temporarily to the DOS shell where you can execute any DOS command. To return to *FEST* from the DOS shell, type *exit* at the DOS prompt.

    Swapping between *FEST* and DOS environments is a very useful option particularly if you want to perform some housekeeping tasks such as locating a file in some directory, copying files, changing an existing extension of some knowledge-base file name to ".rul", or even if you would like to perform other non-related tasks such as using electronic mail.

The *K-Base* option allows you to manipulate any one of *FEST*'s knowledge bases. Each knowledge base is associated with nine unique files. Two of these files, the *synonym file* and the *membership function file*, are discussed in detail in Chapter 8 and, therefore, we also defer to Chapter 8 the discussion of the main menu items *Synonym* and *M-Function*.

The nine files associated with each knowledge base are as follows.

1.  The *knowledge base file*, whose extension is ".rul", contains the knowledge base provided by the user.

2.  The *keywords and synonyms file*, whose extension is ".kwd", contains the keywords and their synonyms.

3.  The *parsed premises file*, whose extension is ".pre", contains the parsed premises of the rules.

4.  The *parsed conclusions file*, whose extension is ".con", contains the parsed conclusions of the rules.

5.  The *relational list file*, whose extension is ".mat", contains the relational list.

6.  The *grammar* file, whose extension is ".grm", contains the grammar for the knowledge base.

7.  The *configuration file*, whose extension is ".cfg", contains the configuration (global parameters) of the given knowledge base.

8.  The *membership functions file*, whose extension is ".mbr", contains the definitions of the membership functions.

9.  The *modifiers file*, whose extension is ".mmd", contains the modifiers defined for the membership functions.

Various other data files are associated with the knowledge base and are loaded when the knowledge base is loaded. These files contain data structures and other software parameters, however their description is beyond the scope of this book.

The main menu item *Grammar* is one of *FEST*'s unique features. It allows you to create a new grammar, or update the grammar currently used by *FEST*. You can, therefore, change the grammar of the knowledge base *dynamically*. Since each knowledge base is associated with a *unique* grammar, this feature enhances considerably the flexibility and power of the expert system tool.

When you choose *Grammar* from the main menu, you invoke the sub-menu shown in Figure 2.3 whose functions include parsing and maintaining lists such as modifier and article lists. We will describe the grammar functions in more detail in Chapter 8.

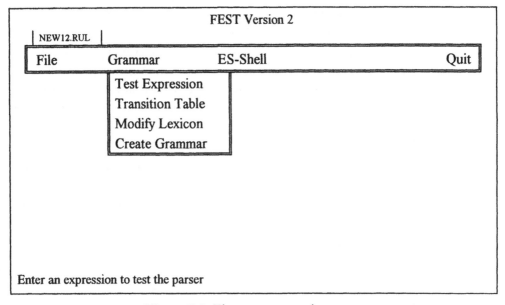

**Figure 2.3** The grammar environment

The third main menu item is the *ES-Shell*, which invokes the *expert system shell* that contains the inference engine which is the heart of the expert system. The *ES-Shell* sub-menu shown in Figure 2.4 consists of six options that are introduced here but whose detailed description is deferred to Chapter 11.

- *Input Data*: This option provides the means for entering the data needed for the inference process and for placing the data on the blackboard. The data can be entered manually by the user, or the data can be obtained from an input device. In the latter case, the data from the input device must first be converted into a DATA file (see the discussion in Section 2.1 pertaining to the execution of *FEST* along with the parameter DATA) whose format *must* conform to the user-defined grammar of particular knowledge base.

- *Infer*: This option invokes the inference engine.

- *Display Blackboard*: This option displays the blackboard.

- *Display Conclusion*: This option displays the conclusion list.

- *Explain*: This option invokes the explanation program to explain the reasoning path of the inference engine.

- *Clear Blackboard*: This option allows you to clear the blackboard.

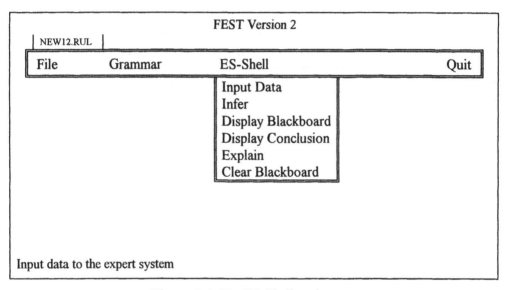

**Figure 2.4**  The ES-Shell environment

The last main menu item is *Quit*. The selection of this option instructs *FEST* to close all the open files, save the changes made to the various files, and to return control to the DOS shell subject to confirmation by the user. To this end, note that FEST displays the following message: *"Shutting down file system. Please Wait."*

Note that *QUIT* is different from the *DOS* sub-menu item (under *File*) introduced earlier in this section. With the latter you are able to swap control between the *FEST* and DOS environments without terminating *FEST*'s current session. In contrast, the selection of *Quit* causes *FEST* to terminate the current session altogether.

Among the files closed by *FEST* when *Quit* is selected are the nine files described above, as well as other files associated with the knowledge base that contain data structures and parameter lists. Additionally, *FEST* also saves in the SYSTEM subdirectory all the lists associated with the grammar, which include the lists of *articles*, *modifiers*, *prepositions*, and *verbs*.

## 2.3 The Editor

Text input is accomplished via the *FEST* editor whose line editing and browsing commands are listed in Table 2.1. *Editing* is a process that allows you to input or modify data, in addition to viewing the data. *Browsing* is a process that allows you to view data, but not to change them.

**Table 2.1** Editor Commands

| Command | Keypad/Arrow | E | B | Description |
|:---:|:---|:---:|:---:|:---|
|  | Home | X |  | Move cursor to beginning of line |
|  |  |  | X | Move to beginning of listing |
|  | End | X |  | Move cursor to end of line |
|  |  |  | X | Move cursor to end of listing |
|  | PgUp |  | X | Move cursor up one screenful |
|  | PgDn |  | X | Move cursor down one screenful |
| ^E | Up arrow |  | X | Move cursor up one line |
| ^X | Down arrow |  | X | Move cursor down one line |
| ^A |  | X |  | Move cursor left one word |
| ^S | Left arrow | X |  | Move cursor left one character |
| ^D | Right arrow | X |  | Move cursor right one character |
| ^F |  | X |  | Move cursor right one word |
| ^V | Ins | X |  | Toggle insert on/off |
| ^G |  | X |  | Delete character under cursor |
|  | Backspace | X |  | Delete character to left of cursor |
|  | ESC | X | X | Terminate editing, option to save |
| ^M | ENTER | X |  | Terminate editing, save changes |

The editor has two main functions:
- To provide a user-friendly text editing environment.
- To check that the text input is syntactically correct.

In *FEST*, the editor combines a full screen browser and a line editor. This means that you may browse through any file but can edit only one line at a time because the editor is linked to the parser and to other data structures of *FEST*. Hence, after editing, *FEST* must parse the new information, check its validity, and store it in the proper data structure.

In Table 2.1, an "X" in column E signifies that the command is applicable to editing, whereas an "X" in column B indicates that the command is applicable to browsing. The caret (^) in Table 2.1 means that you should press *and hold* the **Ctrl** key and then press the indicated letter key. Notice that some commands can be issued either through the sequence indicated in the **Command** column, or by using the keys listed under the **Keypad/Arrow** column.

To terminate the editing process, you can use either the **ESC** key or the **ENTER** key, or use the mouse. The **ESC** key terminates the editing session without saving the changes made, whereas the **ENTER** key terminates the editing session while saving the changes made and/or any newly entered data.

# 3 FUZZY SET THEORY

Classical set theory establishes systematic relations among objects within a set as well as between elements of various sets. A *set* is a collection of any number of definite, well distinguished objects, called the *elements* of the set, that share common properties. Thus, an object may either belong to the set or be completely excluded from it. In other words, if $A$ is a set and $x$ is an element, then $x$ belongs to $A$, $x \in A$, if and only if $x$ satisfies all the membership requirements of $A$; otherwise $x \notin A$.

For example, if A is the set of people who are 40 years old, then for $x$ to belong to $A$, $x$ *must be* 40. However, if $x$ is 39.9 years old, this person will be excluded from $A$. Since there is no indication of how close the rejected $x$ came to being an element of $A$, a 5 year old child will be rejected from the set $A$ just the same as the 39.9 years old person. Classifying the 5 year old child and the 39.9 year old person in the same category, while at the same time classifying the 40 year old and the 39.9 year old into two different categories, clearly demonstrates the kind of inconsistencies associated with classical set theory.

Classical set theory has contributed greatly to the development of a wide range of scientific applications in areas where decision making is necessary (e.g., medicine, business, and engineering). Methods based on classical set theory are utilized mainly in areas where measurements can be made very precisely. However, when such favourable conditions are not reflected in the domain of the problem, the application of classical set theory does not yield good results.

Thus, the use of classical set theory to classify data and knowledge may lead to distortion in the interpretation of the data and knowledge. Sometimes, the transition from membership in one set to membership in another set is not abrupt, but gradual. In such cases, classifying elements in terms of crisp sets implies arbitrarily drawn boundaries between the sets. The problem is even more severe in cases where the information available for the decision making process is difficult to obtain in precise mathematical form, and therefore, the decision must be made based on data containing some degree of error.

These observations led to the development of *Fuzzy Set Theory*, first introduced by Lotfi A. Zadeh [108]. Fuzzy set theory differs from classical set theory in one crucial aspect: *An element can belong to the fuzzy set, be completely excluded from the fuzzy set, or it can belong to the fuzzy set to any intermediate degree between these two extremes*. The extent to which an element belongs to a given fuzzy set is called the *grade of membership* or *degree of membership*. We can say, therefore, that classical set theory is a special case of fuzzy set theory.

The term *fuzzy* was introduced by Zadeh to describe sets whose membership criteria are vague. Thus, *warmish beer* is only marginally a member of the set of cold drinks. Uncertainty about a statement such as *the beer is cold* is not represented by the *probability* that the beer is cold, but rather by what Zadeh calls the *possibility* that the beer is cold. The possibility of a statement is represented by a number generated by a *membership function*. The membership function $\chi$ associated with a fuzzy set assigns degrees of membership to elements in the set. For example, we can assign the following values to the membership function associated with the temperature of beer: the degree of membership of 38°F beer in the fuzzy set of cold beers is 1 ($\chi[38] = 1$), but the degree of membership of 46°F beer is only 0.2 ($\chi[46] = 0.2$).

The use of fuzzy set theory is very appealing in cases where the decision must be made in environments in which the information available is incomplete, vague, or ambiguous. The result, referred to as the *certainty factor* (CF) which is computed for each decision process, represents the *degree of belief* that the decision reached is correct. Note that although the certainty factor can have a value in any range, it is commonly normalized to the interval [0,1].

## 3.1 Mathematical Preliminaries

Let us begin by defining the notion of a fuzzy set.

*Definition 3.1.1*: Let $U$ be the universe of discourse and let $u$ designate the generic element of $U$. A fuzzy set $F$ of $U$ is characterized by a membership function $\chi_F: U \rightarrow [0,1]$, which associates with each element $u \in U$ a number $\chi_F(u)$ representing the grade of membership of $u$ in $F$, and is designated as:

$$F = \{(u, \chi_F(u)) \mid u \in U\}$$

Consider for example the fuzzy set TALL [7]. The elements of the set are men whose membership grades depend on their heights. For example, a man who is 5 feet tall might have a membership degree of 0, a man who is 7 feet tall might have a membership degree of 1, and men of intermediate heights have intermediate grades of membership between 0 and 1. Since different individuals may have differing opinions as to whether a given man is tall, there is a plurality of possible representations for the set TALL. One such representation is shown in Table 3.1.

**Table 3.1** Fuzzy set TALL

| Height | Grade of Membership |
|--------|---------------------|
| 5'0"   | 0.00                |
| 5'4"   | 0.08                |
| 5'8"   | 0.32                |
| 6'0"   | 0.50                |
| 6'4"   | 0.82                |
| 6'8"   | 0.98                |
| 7'0"   | 1.00                |

According to this representation, the fuzzy set TALL is defined by its domain, the set of heights, {5'0", 5'4", 5'8", 6'0", 6'4", 6'8", 7'0"} and the corresponding degrees of membership {0.00, 0.08, 0.32, 0.50, 0.82, 0.98, 1.00}. Thus, the fuzzy set is an association between numbers, a correspondence that assigns to a given height one and only one number in the unit interval. Remember, however, that the fuzzy set is a subjective evaluation applied to heights to obtain degrees of membership. We can symbolize the fuzzy set TALL in the following way:

$$TALL : Heights \rightarrow [0,1]$$

where *Heights* designates the domain of TALL and [0,1] is the co-domain.

The tabular representation of the grades of membership in Table 3.1 depicts the fuzzy set TALL as having a discrete, *finite universe of discourse*. The set can also be represented in graphical form as shown in Figure 3.1. However, the problem with these representations is that intermediate height values are not accounted for (e.g., the heights 5'2", 6'3", etc.). To solve this problem, we need to interpolate a value for the grade of membership if the height is not provided by the table (or graph).

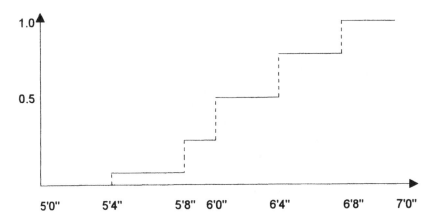

**Figure 3.1** Graphical representation of TALL

There are many methods to perform interpolations. We can use the piecewise-linear interpolation shown in Figure 3.2, or use a smoothing function, called the *S-function*, which is defined as:

$$S(x; \alpha, \beta, \gamma) = \begin{cases} 0 & \text{for } x \le \alpha \\ 2(\dfrac{x-\alpha}{\gamma-\alpha})^2 & \text{for } \alpha < x < \beta \\ 1-2(\dfrac{x-\gamma}{\gamma-\alpha})^2 & \text{for } \beta < x < \gamma \\ 1 & \text{for } x \ge \gamma \end{cases} \tag{3.1}$$

where $\alpha$ and $\gamma$ are the function's end points, and $\beta = (\alpha + \gamma)/2$ is referred to as the *crossover point* [45].

Another often used membership function has a "bell shape" and is referred to as the $\pi$-function [45]:

$$\pi(x; \beta, \gamma) = \begin{cases} S(x; \gamma-\beta, \ \gamma-\beta/2, \ \gamma) & \text{for } x \le \gamma \\ 1-S(x; \gamma, \ \gamma+\beta/2, \ \beta+\gamma) & \text{for } x > \gamma \end{cases} \tag{3.2}$$

where $S(x; \cdot, \cdot, \cdot)$ is the *S-function* given in Equation (3.1). In Equation (3.2), the parameter $\gamma$ is the point at which $\pi$ is unity, and the parameter $\beta$ represents the distance between the two crossover points of $\pi$ (resulting from the two *S-functions, S* and $1-S$) and is referred to as the *bandwidth* of the $\pi$-function.

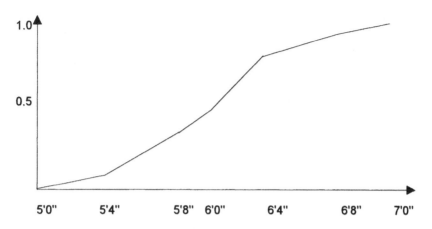

**Figure 3.2** Piecewise-linear interpolation for TALL

Fuzzy sets are characterized by their *support* and *height*. The following definitions introduce these notions as well as the notion of a *normal* fuzzy set.

*Definition 3.1.2*: The *support* of the fuzzy set $F$ is the set of points in the universe of discourse $U$ for which $\chi_F(u)$ is positive.

*Definition 3.1.3*: The *height* of the fuzzy set $F$ is the supremum of $\chi_F(u)$ over the universe of discourse $U$, namely:

$$hgt(F) = sup_{u \in U}(\chi_F(u))$$

The height of a fuzzy set allows us to classify the fuzzy set as normal or subnormal.

*Definition 3.1.4*: A fuzzy set $F$ is said to be *normal* if its height is unity, that is, if

$$sup_{u \in U}(\chi_F(u)) = 1$$

Otherwise, $F$ is called *subnormal*.

To illustrate these concepts, refer to Table 3.1 where it can be seen that the *support* of the fuzzy set TALL is the set {5'4", 5'8", 6'0", 6'4", 6'8, 7'0"}, and its *height* is $hgt$(TALL) = 1. Therefore, TALL is a *normal* fuzzy set.

Normal fuzzy sets play an important role in fuzzy expert systems because membership functions are utilized in the *inference process*. If the set is subnormal, the inference engine may never reach certain conclusions. Note, however, that any subnormal fuzzy set may be normalized by dividing $\chi_F$ by $hgt(F)$.

**Example 3.1:** Consider the set $U = \{a, b, c, d, e\}$ and assume a fuzzy subset $A$ of $U$ represented as $A = 0.3/a + 0.6/b + 0.9/c + 0.5/d$. This type of fuzzy set symbolic representation asserts that element $a$ has a grade of membership 0.3, $b$ has a grade of membership 0.6, *c* has a grade of membership 0.9, and *d* has a grade of membership 0.5. Note that in this representation, the symbol + plays the role of union and does not imply arithmetic sum.

Since all the grades of membership are positive, the *support* of $A=\{a, b, c, d\}$. The *height* of *A* is $hgt(A) = 0.9$ and therefore the set *A* is a *subnormal* fuzzy set. To normalize *A*, we divide the grades of membership by $hgt(A)$, yielding the *normal* fuzzy set:

$$\tilde{A} = \frac{1}{3}/a + \frac{2}{3}/b + 1/c + \frac{5}{9}/d$$

The next three examples illustrate the construction of membership functions.

**Example 3.2:** The membership function of the fuzzy set *B* in the universe labeled COLD can be defined in terms of the *S-function* given below and the corresponding graph shown in Figure 3.3:

$$\chi_B(x) = 1 - S(x;30,45,60) = \begin{cases} 1 & \text{for } x \leq 30 \\ 1 - 2(\frac{x-30}{30})^2 & \text{for } 30 < x < 45 \\ 2(\frac{x-60}{30})^2 & \text{for } 45 < x < 60 \\ 0 & \text{for } x \geq 60 \end{cases}$$

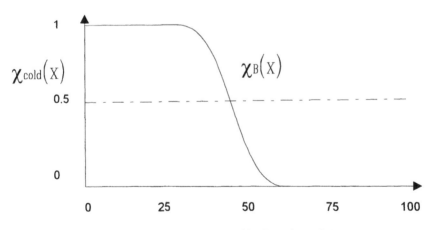

**Figure 3.3** Membership function of COLD

**Example 3.3:** Assume that *U* is countable and consider the fuzzy set *A*, referred to as SMALL, whose membership function is given by:

$$\chi_A(u) = \sum_a^c (1 + (\frac{u}{a+b})^2)^{-1} / u$$

Note that the *support* of A is the (discrete) interval [a, c] and that this type of fuzzy set symbolic representation is a simple extension of the one shown in Example 3.1.

We see that the membership function is monotonically decreasing with $\chi_A(a)$ = 1 and $\lim_{c \to \infty} \chi_A(c) = 0$. If we let a = 0, c = ∞, and b = 10, we get the following definition of the fuzzy set SMALL:

$$\chi_{OLD} = \int_{50}^{100} (1 + (\frac{u-50}{5})^{-2})^{-1} / u$$

with sample values given in the following table:

| u | 0 | 1 | 3 | 5 | 7 | 10 | 12 | 15 |
|---|---|---|---|---|---|----|----|----|
| $\chi_{SMALL}$ | 1.00 | 0.99 | 0.91 | 0.80 | 0.67 | 0.50 | 0.41 | 0.31 |

**Example 3.4:** Let $U = (u \mid 0 \leq u \leq 100)$ represent age in years. Thus, the universe of discourse U is a continuum and the fuzzy set A, labeled OLD, may be expressed in terms of the function:

$$\chi_A(u) = \int_a^c (1 + (\frac{u-a}{b-a})^{-2})^{-1} / u$$

This type of fuzzy set symbolic representation is interpreted similarly to the one in Example 3.2, with the integral sign replacing the summation symbol and playing the role of union over the continuum rather than integration.

We note that the membership function is a monotonically increasing function over the support interval [a, c] with $\chi_A(a) = 0$ and $\lim_{c \to \infty} \chi_A(c) = 1$. If, for example, we let the support be the interval [50, 100] and b = 55, then the definition of OLD becomes:

$$\chi_{OLD} = \int_{50}^{100} (1 + (\frac{u-50}{5})^{-2})^{-1} / u$$

Other types of standard membership functions which are advantageous in specific applications of fuzzy sets can be found in references [65, 70].

## 3.2 Algebra Of Fuzzy Sets

We can now discuss several basic operations on fuzzy sets. We will first consider the operation of *complementation*. In classical set theory, the complement of a set contains all the elements that are not in the original set. In fuzzy set theory, however, complementation takes into account the grades of membership of the elements in the set. The complement of a fuzzy set is defined as the set whose grades of membership are exactly 1 minus the grades of membership of the complemented set.

*Definition 3.2.1*: The *complement* of a fuzzy set $A$, denoted by $\sim\!A$, is defined as:

$$\sim\!A = \int_U [1 - \chi_A(u)]/u$$

Often, the complement $\sim\!A$ of the fuzzy set $A$ is denoted as *NOT* A.

To illustrate the complementation operation, consider the representations of the fuzzy sets TALL and NOT TALL shown in Table 3.2. As we can see, if $x$ has a grade of membership $\chi$ in the set TALL, then it has a grade of membership $1 - \chi$ in the set NOT TALL.

The example in Table 3.2 points to an important observation. Ask yourself, what is implied by the statement *John is not tall?* In classical set theory, this would imply that John can be anything *but* tall. However, in fuzzy set theory, this implies that John is not tall but, *at the same time*, that John may be *tall, more or less tall*, even *very tall* - all to some varying degrees - as well as that John may be of *medium height* also to some degree. In other words, John can be affiliated with the fuzzy sets TALL, VERY_ TALL, MORE_OR_LESS_TALL, etc., albeit with different grades of membership in each of these fuzzy sets [84]. We will return to this observation in Chapter 7 where we discuss knowledge processing.

**Table 3.2** Complementation

| TALL | | NOT TALL | |
|---|---|---|---|
| 5'0" | 0.00 | 5'0" | 1.00 |
| 5'4" | 0.08 | 5'4" | 0.92 |
| 5'8" | 0.32 | 5'8" | 0.68 |
| 6'0" | 0.50 | 6'0" | 0.50 |
| 6'4" | 0.82 | 6'4" | 0.18 |
| 6'8" | 0.98 | 6'8" | 0.02 |
| 7'0" | 1.00 | 7'0" | 0.00 |

Let us now consider the *intersection* operation. In classical set theory, the intersection of two sets contains those elements of the two sets that are in one set *and* in the other. However, in fuzzy set theory, an element of a fuzzy set may be partly in one set and partly in another. Therefore, the statement that an element is in the intersection of two fuzzy sets cannot be more true than stating that the element is in either one. Thus, at any point in the domain, the truth of the proposition that an element is in the fuzzy set TALL *and* NOT TALL is the *minimum* of the truth of the propositions that the element is in TALL and that it is in NOT TALL. In other words:

$$\chi_{\text{TALL }and\text{ NOT TALL}} = min\ (\chi_{\text{TALL}},\ \chi_{\text{NOT TALL}})$$

*Definition 3.2.2*: The *intersection* of the fuzzy sets $A$ and $B$, denoted by $A \cap B$ (or $A$ AND $B$) is defined by:

$$A \cap B = \int_U [\chi_A(x)\ \&\ \chi_B(x)]/x, \qquad x \in U$$

where the symbol & stands for *min*. Thus, for any $a \in A$ and $b \in B$,

$$min[\chi_A(a),\ \chi_B(b)] = \chi_A(a) \quad \text{if } \chi_A(a) \le \chi_B(b)$$

$$= \chi_B(b) \quad \text{if } \chi_A(a) > \chi_B(b)$$

Refer again to the fuzzy sets TALL and NOT TALL given in Table 3.2. Intuitively, we can say that because TALL is equivalent to NOT SHORT, then NOT SHORT and NOT TALL correspond to MIDDLE-SIZED. Therefore, a person who is *tall* AND *not tall* is actually *middle-sized*. Thus, we expect the highest membership degree of the intersection of TALL and NOT TALL to be in the middle of the domain and the lowest membership degree to be at the edges, as shown in Table 3.3.

**Table 3.3** Fuzzy set MIDDLE-SIZED

| TALL | | | NOT TALL | | | MIDDLE-SIZED | |
|---|---|---|---|---|---|---|---|
| 5'0" | 0.00 | | 5'0" | 1.00 | | 5'0" | 0.00 |
| 5'4" | 0.08 | | 5'4" | 0.92 | | 5'4" | 0.08 |
| 5'8" | 0.32 | *AND* | 5'8" | 0.68 | $\Rightarrow$ | 5'8" | 0.32 |
| 6'0" | 0.50 | | 6'0" | 0.50 | | 6'0" | 0.50 |
| 6'4" | 0.82 | | 6'4" | 0.18 | | 6'4" | 0.18 |
| 6'8" | 0.98 | | 6'8" | 0.02 | | 6'8" | 0.02 |
| 7'0" | 1.00 | | 7'0" | 0.00 | | 7'0" | 0.00 |

The operation of *union* of two fuzzy sets is the set of those elements that belong either to one of the constituent sets or to both. For any point in the domain of the two fuzzy sets, the membership grades of the elements of the union set must be equal to the greater of the two membership grades of the elements of either one of the constituent sets. Thus,

$$\chi_{\text{TALL or NOT TALL}} = max \, (\chi_{\text{TALL}}, \chi_{\text{NOT TALL}})$$

*Definition 3.2.3*: The *union* of the fuzzy sets $A$ and $B$, denoted by $A \cup B$ (or *A OR B*) is defined by:

$$A \cup B = \int_U \, [\chi_A(x) \, \# \, \chi_B(x)]/x, \qquad x \in U$$

where the symbol # stands for *max*. Thus, for any $a \in A$ and $b \in B$,

$$max[\chi_A(a), \chi_B(b)] = \chi_A(a) \qquad \text{if } \chi_A(a) \geq \chi_B(b)$$

$$= \chi_B(b) \qquad \text{if } \chi_A(a) < \chi_B(b)$$

Table 3.4 illustrates the operation of *union* applied to the fuzzy sets TALL and NOT TALL. A person who is *tall* or *short* (*not tall*) is *not middle-sized*. As can be seen, the membership function of NOT MIDDLE-SIZED attains the highest values at the edges of the domain, and the smallest value at the centre.

**Table 3.4** Fuzzy set NOT MIDDLE-SIZED

| TALL | | | NOT TALL | | | NOT MIDDLE-SIZED | |
|---|---|---|---|---|---|---|---|
| 5'0" | 0.00 | | 5'0" | 1.00 | | 5'0" | 1.00 |
| 5'4" | 0.08 | | 5'4" | 0.92 | | 5'4" | 0.92 |
| 5'8" | 0.32 | | 5'8" | 0.68 | | 5'8" | 0.68 |
| 6'0" | 0.50 | *OR* | 6'0" | 0.50 | $\Rightarrow$ | 6'0" | 0.50 |
| 6'4" | 0.82 | | 6'4" | 0.18 | | 6'4" | 0.82 |
| 6'8" | 0.98 | | 6'8" | 0.02 | | 6'8" | 0.98 |
| 7'0" | 1.00 | | 7'0" | 0.00 | | 7'0" | 1.00 |

It is simple to justify the choice of the *max* and *min* operations in the definitions of union and intersection, respectively. These operators are the only ones that exhibit the following necessary properties [71]:

1. The membership degrees in the compound fuzzy set depend only on the membership degrees in the constituent fuzzy sets that form it.

2. The operators *max* and *min* are commutative, associative, and mutually distributive.

3. The operators *max* and *min* are continuous and non-decreasing with respect to each of their arguments.

4. Complete membership in TALL and in SHORT implies complete membership in TALL *AND* SHORT. Complete lack of membership implies complete lack of membership in TALL *OR* SHORT.

The following properties follow from the definitions of *complementation, intersection,* and *union.* Let $X$, $Y$, and $Z$ be fuzzy sets and let $x \in X$, $y \in Y$, and $z \in Z$, then:

*Commutativity:*
$$\chi_X(x) \cup \chi_Y(y) = \chi_Y(y) \cup \chi_X(x)$$
$$\chi_X(x) \cap \chi_Y(y) = \chi_Y(y) \cap \chi_X(x)$$

*Associativity:*
$$[\chi_X(x) \cup \chi_Y(y)] \cup \chi_Z(z) = \chi_X(x) \cup [\chi_Y(y) \cup \chi_Z(z)]$$
$$[\chi_X(x) \cap \chi_Y(y)] \cap \chi_Z(z) = \chi_X(x) \cap [\chi_Y(y) \cap \chi_Z(z)]$$

*Idempotency:*
$$\chi_X(x) \cup \chi_X(x) = \chi_X(x)$$
$$\chi_X(x) \cap \chi_X(x) = \chi_X(x)$$

*Distributivity:*
$$\chi_X(x) \cup [\chi_Y(y) \cap \chi_Z(z)] = [\chi_X(x) \cup \chi_Y(y)] \cap [\chi_X(x) \cup \chi_Z(z)]$$
$$\chi_X(x) \cap [\chi_Y(y) \cup \chi_Z(z)] = [\chi_X(x) \cap \chi_Y(y)] \cup [\chi_X(x) \cap \chi_Z(z)]$$

*Absorption:*
$$\chi_X(x) \cup [\chi_X(x) \cap \chi_Y(y)] = \chi_X(x)$$
$$\chi_X(x) \cap [\chi_X(x) \cup \chi_Y(y)] = \chi_X(x)$$

*DeMorgan's Laws:*
$$\sim[\chi_X(x) \cap \chi_Y(y)] = \sim\chi_X(x) \cup \sim\chi_Y(y)$$
$$\sim[\chi_X(x) \cup \chi_Y(y)] = \sim\chi_X(x) \cap \sim\chi_Y(y)$$

*Identity:*
$$\chi_X(x) \cup X_\Phi = \chi_X(x)$$
$$\chi_X(x) \cap X_\Phi = \chi_X(x)$$
where $X_\Phi$ designates the membership grade of the empty fuzzy set.

*Involution:*
$$\sim[\sim\chi_X(x)] = \chi_X(x)$$

To conclude this chapter, let us introduce two additional concepts. The first, given by Definition 3.2.4, refers to the convex combination of fuzzy sets. The second, considered in Definition 3.2.5, is concerned with the product of fuzzy sets.

*Definition 3.2.4*: Let $A_1$, $A_2$, ..., $A_n$ be fuzzy subsets in the universes of discourse $U_1$, $U_2$, ..., $U_n$, respectively, and let $\omega_1$, $\omega_2$, ..., $\omega_n$ be non-negative weights such that $\sum_{i=1}^{n} \omega_i = 1$. Then, the *convex combination* of $A_1$, $A_2$, ..., $A_n$ is the fuzzy set $A$ whose membership function is defined by:

$$\chi_A = \omega_1 \chi_{A_1} + \omega_2 \chi_{A_2} + .... + \omega_n \chi_{A_n}$$

where the symbol + denotes the arithmetic sum.

The concept of convex combination is useful in the representation of linguistic hedges such as *essentially*, *typically*, etc., which modify the weights. The weights can also be interpreted as coefficients of importance of the components of the fuzzy set $A$ constructed from the fuzzy sets $A_1$, $A_2$, ..., $A_n$. The following examples illustrate the concept of convex combination.

**Example 3.5:** Let $U_1 = (u_1 \mid 10 \leq u_1 \leq 250)$ where $u_1$ represents weight in kilograms. The fuzzy set $A_1$, labeled HEAVY, may be expressed as:

$$\text{HEAVY} = \int_{40}^{100} (1 + (\frac{u_1 - 40}{30})^{-2})^{-1} / u_1$$

Let $U_2 = (u_2 \mid 50 \leq u_2 \leq 220)$ where $u_2$ represents height in centimetres. The fuzzy set $A_2$, labeled TALL, may be defined as:

$$\text{TALL} = \int_{140}^{190} (1 + (\frac{u_2 - 140}{30})^{-2})^{-1} / u_2$$

Then, the fuzzy set $A$, labeled BIG, may be defined as a convex combination of the fuzzy sets HEAVY and TALL, such that:

$$\text{BIG} = 0.6\text{HEAVY} + 0.4\text{TALL}$$

with

$$\chi_A(u_1, u_2) = \int_{40}^{100} \int_{140}^{190} [0.6\chi_{A_1}(u_1) + 0.4\chi_{A_2}(u_2)] / (u_1, u_2)$$

**Example 3.6:** Consider the following valuations for the fuzzy set BIG introduced in the previous example:

$$\chi_{\text{BIG}}(70,170) = 0.6\chi_{\text{HEAVY}}(70) + 0.4\chi_{\text{TALL}}(170)$$
$$= 0.6 \times 0.5 + 0.4 \times 0.5$$
$$= 0.50$$

$$\chi_{BIG}(80,170) = 0.6\chi_{HEAVY}(80) + 0.4\chi_{TALL}(170)$$
$$= 0.6 \times 0.64 + 0.4 \times 0.5$$
$$= 0.584$$

$$\chi_{BIG}(70,180) = 0.6\chi_{HEAVY}(70) + 0.4\chi_{TALL}(180)$$
$$= 0.6 \times 0.5 + 0.4 \times 0.64$$
$$= 0.556$$

These results indicate that the variations in weight have a stronger influence on the membership function of the fuzzy set BIG than the variations in height. This is due to our assignment of greater "importance" to the component HEAVY in determining the fuzzy set BIG as a convex combination of HEAVY and TALL.

The notion of *product* of fuzzy sets defined below is useful to the process of evaluating fuzzy production rules and is described in Chapter 10.

*Definition 3.2.5*: The *product* of the fuzzy sets $A$ and $B$, denoted by $AB$, is defined as:

$$AB = \int_U (\chi_A(u) \cdot \chi_B(u))/u$$

Following this definition we can also define $A^p$, where $p$ is any positive number:

$$A^p = \int_U (\chi_A(u))^p / u$$

Similarly, if $\omega$ is any non-negative real number such that $\omega \cdot hgt(A) \leq 1$, then:

$$\omega A = \int_U (\omega \cdot \chi_A(u))/u$$

# 4 POSSIBILITY/PROBABILITY CONSISTENCY PRINCIPLE

Possibility theory was introduced by Zadeh [115] in 1978 to model possible events based on the theories of fuzzy logic and fuzzy sets. To illustrates the relation between fuzziness and possibility, consider first the following non-fuzzy statement which we refer to as proposition $p$:

$$p : X \text{ is an integer in the interval } [0, 5]$$

The interpretation of proposition $p$ asserts that:

1. $X$ can assume any integer value in the interval $[0, 5]$.
2. Any integer outside of the interval $[0, 5]$ cannot be a value of $X$.

Hence, proposition $p$ induces a *possibility distribution* $\Pi(X)$ which associates with each integer $u \in [0, 5]$ the possibility that $u$ can be a value of $X$:

$$\Pi_X = \begin{cases} Poss(X = u) = 1 & \text{for } 0 \leq u \leq 5 \\ Poss(X = u) = 0 & \text{otherwise} \end{cases}$$

where *Poss* $(X = u)$ stands for *the possibility that $X$ may assume the integer value $u$.*

Consider now a fuzzified version of proposition $p$ which we refer to as proposition $q$:

$$q : X \text{ is a small integer in the interval } [0, 5]$$

where *small integer* is the fuzzy set defined by:

SMALL_INTEGER = *1/0 + 1/1 + 0.9/2 + 0.7/3 + 0.5/4 + 0.2/5*

Recall that this type of fuzzy set symbolic representation (see Example 3.1) asserts that the grade of membership of the integer *3* in the fuzzy set SMALL_INTEGER is *0.7* (or, equivalently, that the strength of the statement *3 is a small integer* is *0.7*), the grade of membership of the integer *5* is *0.2*, etc.

Consequently, we can interpret proposition *q* by saying that any integer in the interval [0, 5] may be a *small integer*, and that the possibility of $X$ assuming the value *u* depends on the grade of membership of *u* in the fuzzy set SMALL_INTEGER. In other words, proposition *q* induces a possibility distribution $\Pi_X$ that associates, with each integer $u \in [0, 5]$, a possibility that *u* can be a value of $X$ which is equal to the grade of membership of *u* in the fuzzy set SMALL_INTEGER. Thus,

$$Poss(X = 0) = Poss(X = 1) = 1$$
$$Poss(X = 2) = 0.9$$
$$Poss(X = 3) = 0.7$$
$$Poss(X = 4) = 0.5$$
$$Poss(X = 5) = 0.2$$
$$Poss(X = u) = 0.0 \ for \ u < 0 \ or \ u > 5$$

As can be seen, the possibility distribution $\Pi_X$ implies that the *degree of possibility* may be any number in the interval [0, 1] rather than only *1* (possible) or *0* (impossible) in the non-fuzzy case. This provides the means for expressing intermediate degrees of possibility which are implicit in commonly encountered propositions such as "it is *slightly possible* that Tom will travel to France", "there is a *high possibility* that a meteor will hit Earth," and so on.

It can be argued that possibility is nothing other than probability in disguise and that, for example, *high possibility* is equivalent to *high probability*. Indeed, such substitution is frequently made in everyday conversation; however, as we show in the following section, the two are not equivalent.

## 4.1 Possibility - Probability Relation

Possibility and probability are two techniques for representing and manipulating uncertainty or imprecision. Let us illustrate the difference between probability and possibility using two examples.

**Example 4.1:** Suppose that a family of seven owns a four-seat car, and consider the question "*how many passengers can ride in the car?*" This question corresponds to the statement "*X passengers ride in the car*", where $X$ takes values in *U = (1, 2, ...., 7)*.

We can associate a possibility distribution with $X$ by letting $Poss(X = u)$ designate the degree of comfort with which $u$ passengers can fit into the car. We can also associate a probability distribution with $X$ by letting $Prob(X = u)$ be the probability that $u$ people will ride in the car. Let us assume that the values of $Poss(X = u)$ and $Prob(X = u)$ have been assessed subjectively and are shown in Table 4.1.

**Table 4.1** Possibility and probability distributions

| $u$ | 1 | 2 | 3 | 4 | 5 | 6 | 7 |
|---|---|---|---|---|---|---|---|
| $Poss\ (X = u)$ | 1 | 1 | 1 | 1 | 0.4 | 0.1 | 0 |
| $Prob\ (X = u)$ | 0.3 | 0.4 | 0.2 | 0.1 | 0 | 0 | 0 |

Table 4.1 exhibits some of the intrinsic differences between possibility and probability. While the probabilities have to sum to $1$ over $U$, the possibility values are not so restricted. Also notice that the possibility that $3$ passengers will ride in the car is $1$ whereas the corresponding probability, $0.2$, is quite small. Thus, high possibility does not necessarily imply high probability, nor does a low degree of probability imply a low degree of possibility. Nevertheless, if the possibility of an event becomes small, then its probability would tend to be smaller too, however, the converse is not true. Furthermore, if an event is impossible, it is bound to be improbable.

The heuristic relationship between possibilities and probabilities demonstrated in Example 4.1 is called the *possibility/probability consistency principle* [115]. We note that the imprecision intrinsic in natural languages is *possibilistic* in nature and that possibility theory provides the basis for dealing with it in a systematic way.

**Example 4.2:** Consider the statement "*John is old*" and let the fuzzy set OLD be subjectively defined on $U = (u \mid 0 \leq u \leq 100)$. Further, assume that the possibility distribution of OLD has the sample values shown in Table 4.2.

**Table 4.2** Possibility distribution of OLD

| $u$ | 10 | 20 | 25 | 30 | 35 | 40 | 50 | 60 | ... |
|---|---|---|---|---|---|---|---|---|---|
| $Poss\ (X = u)$ | 0.0 | 0.2 | 0.3 | 0.5 | 0.8 | 0.9 | 1.0 | 1.0 | ... |

Table 4.3 shows the probability distribution of OLD derived by assuming that any age greater than or equal to $60$ is *old*. Note that the values shown in Tables 4.2 and 4.3 are intended for illustration only.

**Table 4.3** Probability distribution of OLD

| $u$ | ... | 40 | 50 | 60 | 70 | 80 | 90 | 100 |
|---|---|---|---|---|---|---|---|---|
| $Prob(X = u)$ | 0.0 | 0.0 | 0.0 | 0.0 | 0.4 | 0.3 | 0.15 | 0.1 | 0.05 |

Tables 4.2 and 4.3 demonstrate an important difference between the concepts and application of possibility and probability. Whereas the probability of some person living to be *100* years old is *0.05*, this statement does not necessarily apply to any specific person. Living to be *100* years old depends among other things on health and physical environment. On the other hand, the possibility distribution provides a subjective tool that enables us to assess the possibility that a specific person will live to be *100* years old.

## 4.2 Possibility Measures

Possibility measures utilize fuzzy sets as a basis for measuring the possibility that an event may or may not happen. Let $A$ be a non-fuzzy subset in $U$ and let $\Pi_X$ be the possibility distribution associated with $X$. Then, the possibility measure of $A$, $\pi(A)$, is defined as [115]:

$$\pi(A) \equiv \sup_{u \in A} \pi_X(u)$$

where $\pi_X(u)$ is the possibility measure of $u$ in $\Pi_X$. More formally, we have the following.

*Definition 4.2.1:* Let $A$ be a fuzzy subset of $U$ characterized by a membership degree $\chi_A$, and let $\Pi_X$ be the possibility distribution associated with a variable $X$ which takes values in $U$. The *possibility measure* of $A$, $\pi(A) = Poss(X = A)$, is defined by:

$$\pi(A) = \sup_{u \in U} [\chi_A(u) \cap \pi_x(u)]$$

Among several possible values, some values are more possible than others, or some are better descriptors of the event. For the value in question, however, there might be no "perfect" or "exact" descriptor.

**Example 4.3:** Consider the domain of HAIR_COLOUR = (*Blond, Red, Brown, Black, White*). Thus, the colour of Bob's hair may be expressed in terms of the possibilistic distribution,

HAIR_COLOUR(Bob) = *0.5/Blond +  0.6/Red + 0.3/Brown*

that can be interpreted by saying that the colour of Bob's hair is a mixture of *blond*, *red*, and *brown* in the ratio *5:6:3*, or as a union of separate descriptors as follows:

*Bob's hair is Blond (is 0.5 possible)*

*Bob's hair is Red (is 0.6 possible)*

*Bob's hair is Brown (is 0.3 possible)*

In the next example we illustrate the use of a membership function in computing the possibility of a fuzzy event.

**Example 4.4:** Suppose that we are interested to know who will be out of town "*around* the middle of the month", and we ask people to give us possible dates of their absence. As a result, we generate the following possibility distributions:

$$\Pi_{Absence}(Bob) = 0.5/16 + 1.0/17 + 0.5/18$$

$$\Pi_{Absence}(Tim) = 0.7/12 + 0.7/13 + 0.7/14 + 1.0/20$$

$$\Pi_{Absence}(Ann) = 0.9/12 + 0.2/16$$

To see how we interpret these possibility distributions, consider Bob for example. He is certain (possibility of *1.0*) that he will be gone on the 17th but it is also possible that he could leave a day earlier or a day later, both with a possibility degree of *0.5*.

Let us define the fuzzy set *middle_of_the_month*, designated by *A*, as follows:

$$\chi_A(u) = 0 \quad for \ 1 \le u \le 10 \ or \ 20 \le u \le 31$$

$$\chi_A(11) = \chi_A(19) = 0.1$$

$$\chi_A(12) = \chi_A(18) = 0.4$$

$$\chi_A(13) = \chi_A(17) = 0.7$$

$$\chi_A(14) = \chi_A(16) = 0.9$$

$$\chi_A(15) = 1$$

We can now use Definition 4.2.1 to derive Bob's possibility measure (the possibility that Bob will be absent during the middle of the month):

$$\pi_{Bob}(A) = max(0.5 \cap 0.9, \ 1.0 \cap 0.7, \ 0.5 \cap 0.4)$$

$$= max(0.5, \ 0.7, \ 0.4)$$

$$= 0.7$$

where $\cap$ stands for the *min* operation.

**Example 4.5:** Let us consider another scenario given by the following possibility distributions:

$$\Pi_{Absence}(Joe) = 1.0/13$$

$$\Pi_{Absence}(Don) = 0.8/13$$

$$\Pi_{Absence}(Eve) = 0.7/13$$

$$\Pi_{Absence}(Jim) = 0.5/13$$

$$\Pi_{Absence}(Ted) = 0.1/13$$

Using the fuzzy set *middle_of_the_month* defined in Example 4.4, we can generate the corresponding possibility measures (namely, the possibilities that each and every one of these people will be absent on the 13th):

$$\pi_{Joe}(A) = max(1.0 \cap 0.7) = 0.7$$

$$\pi_{Don}(A) = max(0.8 \cap 0.7) = 0.7$$

$$\pi_{Eve}(A) = max(0.7 \cap 0.7) = 0.7$$

$$\pi_{Jim}(A) = max(0.5 \cap 0.7) = 0.5$$

$$\pi_{Ted}(A) = max(0.1 \cap 0.7) = 0.1$$

Notice in Example 4.5 that the possibility measures of Joe, Don, and Eve are equal (*0.7*) whereas the possibilities of their absence differ (*1.0, 0.8,* and *0.7,* respectively). This result conflicts with intuition because possibility differences should be reflected in the possibility measures. The problem is due to the use of the *min* ($\cap$) operator in the calculation of the possibility measure. Therefore, it is desirable to have a possibility measure that reflects the interaction between the possibility distribution $\Pi_X$ and the degree of membership $\chi_A$ in the fuzzy set $A$. Hence, the following new definition of possibility measure is introduced:

*Definition 4.2.2:* Let $B$ be a fuzzy subset of $U$ characterized by the membership function $\chi_B$ and let $\Pi_X$ be the possibility distribution associated with the variable $X$ which takes values in $U$. The *possibility measure* of $B$, $\pi(B)$, is defined as:

$$\pi(B) = \sup_{u \in U}[\chi_B(u) \cdot \pi_x(u)]$$

If we apply Definition 4.2.2 to the scenario depicted in Example 4.5, we obtain the following possibility measures:

$$\pi_{Joe}(A) = max(1.0 \times 0.7) = 0.70$$

$$\pi_{Don}(A) = max(0.8 \times 0.7) = 0.56$$

$$\pi_{Eve}(A) = max(0.7 \times 0.7) = 0.49$$

$$\pi_{Jim}(A) = max(0.5 \times 0.7) = 0.35$$

$$\pi_{Ted}(A) = max(0.1 \times 0.7) = 0.07$$

As we can see, these new values have a linear relation to the possibility distribution.

Possibility theory is used in fuzzy expert systems to solve problems in which we have to compute, model, and evaluate fuzzy or possible events. Later in the book, we will describe how to incorporate fuzzy events into fuzzy expert systems, but for now we turn our attention to knowledge representation in the next chapter.

# 5 KNOWLEDGE REPRESENTATION

Knowledge is the trademark of artificial intelligence systems. The process of embedding knowledge within the artificial intelligence system consists of four steps:

- Knowledge Acquisition

- Knowledge Representation

- Knowledge Validation

- Knowledge Generation.

The bulk of this chapter (Section 5.3) is devoted to the discussion of current knowledge representation techniques. In order to put knowledge representation in perspective, we also discuss briefly the processes of acquiring knowledge (Section 5.2), validating knowledge (within Section 5.3), and generating knowledge (Section 5.4). We defer to the next two chapters the issues of fuzziness in the knowledge base and how the fuzzy expert system should handle it.

*Knowledge representation* is a fundamental component in any artificial intelligence system. This component encodes knowledge, objects, goals, and actions, and processes them into data structures and procedures. Moreover, the knowledge representation scheme predicates the reasoning process and its efficiency.

The choice of an appropriate knowledge representation paradigm is of particular importance due to the plurality and variety of existing knowledge representation techniques. Since the representation primitives, together with the process that combines them, effectively limit what the system can perceive, know, or understand, the choice of knowledge representation technique is crucial to the design of intelligent systems that can understand natural languages, characterize conceptual data, or learn about their environment.

## 5.1 What Is Knowledge?

It is often useful to draw a distinction between data and information. *Data* consist of raw figures, measurements, and files that do not necessarily answer questions that the user may have. *Information*, on the other hand, is something more refined. It is often the result of processing crude data, gathering useful statistics about the data, or answering specific questions posed by the user.

In the realm of artificial intelligence, we usually add another source of data, referred to as *knowledge*, and consider it as a refinement of information. Though knowledge can be incomplete or fuzzy, it consists of collections of related facts, procedures, models, and heuristics that can be used in problem-solving or inference systems.

Knowledge may be regarded as *contextual information*, organized so that it can be readily applied to problem-solving, perception, and learning. Knowledge varies widely both in content and appearance, and it may be specific, general, exact, fuzzy, procedural, or declarative [96].

A *knowledge base* is an external file which contains knowledge and facts about the domain of the problem. Knowledge bases are often classified as either procedural or declarative. A *procedural knowledge* base is similar to a computer program in that it is difficult to understand and modify, while a *declarative* knowledge base generally requires wasteful searching. Therefore, most practical knowledge base representations tend to form a hybrid of the two schemes.

Knowledge bases can store various types of information, such as the following[3].

- *Objects*: We can think of knowledge in terms of *facts* about objects in the environment around us. Statements such as *birds have wings* or *snow is white* are examples of facts about the world we live in.

- *Events*: We have knowledge about events and actions around us. Statements such as *Joe kissed Joan in the car* or *it will be cold tonight* are examples which describe actions or events.

- *Performance*: An action like driving a car involves knowledge about *how* to do things. In this case, knowledge can represent a detailed set of instructions on how to drive a car.

- *Meta-knowledge*: We also have knowledge about what we know. For example, we often know about the reliability of certain information, or about the relative importance of specific facts about the world.

In the following sections, we consider the four steps that constitute the process of embedding knowledge within the artificial intelligence system, namely, *acquisition, representation, validation,* and *generation*.

## 5.2 Knowledge Acquisition

Knowledge acquisition is the process of acquiring knowledge from an expert (or experts) [62], and is usually performed by knowledge engineers. The knowledge engineer interviews the expert and gathers all the available knowledge from him or her.

In general, the expert provides the knowledge engineer with two types of knowledge.

1. *Propositions.* Propositions such as *snow is white* and *John is tall* describe knowledge pertaining to the domain in question. They provide facts for the expert system and are stored in a file and loaded onto the blackboard during inferencing.

    Most propositions are in the form of two objects and one relation. For example, in the proposition *snow is white*, both *snow* and *white* are objects while *is* indicates a relation between them. In this case, the relation *is* indicates a property (or characteristic), namely, snow is (usually) characterized by being white.

2. *Rules.* The expert may provide the knowledge engineer with a set of rules that describe certain cause-and-effect situations. Rules are used to infer new propositions from existing propositions [78], and are divided into two parts:

    (a) The *antecedent* ( *If* part) is the conditional part of the rule.

    (b) The *consequent* (*Then* part) is the concluding part of the rule.

    Based on the *modus ponens* law [78], if the conditional part of the rule is true, then the conclusion becomes true. We will return to this assertion in Chapters 9 and 10.

When the knowledge acquisition process is completed, the knowledge engineer has to decide on the method of transforming the knowledge into some form that is both consistent and understood by the expert system. This process, called *knowledge representation*, is considered in the following section.

## 5.3  Knowledge Representation

Knowledge representation is an important step in the process of designing expert systems. To use the types of knowledge described in Section 5.1, we must represent the knowledge in the knowledge base in a form that will be not only efficient to retrieve and manipulate by the expert system but also amenable to the user. The user should be able to maintain, view, edit, and print the knowledge base in a relatively straightforward manner.

Barr and Feigenbaum [3] describe a number of methods to represent knowledge. Three of these methods, *semantic nets, frames*, and *production rules*, are considered in the following paragraphs.

### 5.3.1  Semantic Nets

Semantic nets were originally developed for use as psychological models of human memory. They are now a standard knowledge representation method in expert systems and are used, in particular, to represent propositions.

The semantic net is a *directed graph* consisting of *nodes* and *links*. The links connect the nodes and describe the relations between them whereas the nodes designate objects, concepts, or events. Figure 5.1 illustrates the general structure of a semantic net.

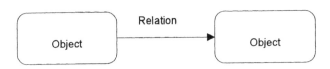

**Figure 5.1**  Structure of semantic net

The links can be defined in a number of ways, depending on the type of knowledge being represented, but usually they represent hierarchies such as *is_a, ako* (which stands for *a kind of*), and *has-part* [3]. For example, the statements,

*dolphins are friendly*

*Flipper is a dolphin*

are represented in Figure 5.2 as a semantic net having three nodes and two links. The nodes are *Flipper, dolphin*, and *friendly*, and the links are *is_a* and *property*.

An important feature of semantic nets is the property of *inheritance*. You have probably noted in the above example that we did not state explicitly that Flipper is friendly but, since the links are hierarchical, Flipper *inherits* the property of friendliness. An immediate advantage of the inheritance property is that some knowledge does not have to be represented *explicitly*. This in turn reduces the amount of knowledge that has to be represented and expedites the search through the knowledge base.

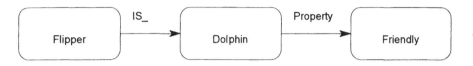

**Figure 5.2** Semantic net example

However, the semantic net knowledge representation scheme has some draw-backs.

1.  *Semantic nets tend to be very large due to duplication of nodes.* For example, consider the following propositions,

    *birds can fly*

    *Robin is a bird*

    whose semantic net representation is shown in Figure 5.3.

**Figure 5.3** Semantic net for robin

Assume that we want to add the ostrich Pikko to the net. Since we know that ostriches are birds which cannot fly, then to incorporate Pikko in the net we have to duplicate the node associated with *bird*, as shown in Figure 5.4.

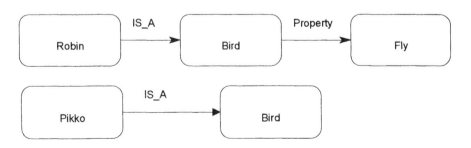

**Figure 5.4** Semantic net for Robin and Pikko

This example illustrates an important issue in semantic nets. Since semantic nets feature the property of inheritance, we must be very careful when linking nodes in the net: the deeper the links, the more specific is the information. We have to duplicate nodes when the specifics do not match the characteristics of the ancestor nodes.

2.   *Semantic nets are difficult to modify.* When we *delete* nodes from the semantic net, we must link the remaining nodes to ensure that information is not lost, inheritance preserved, and that no node is linked to the deleted nodes (resulting in dangling nodes).

If we *insert* new nodes into the net, we must ensure that the semantics of the net are not altered and that inheritance is preserved.

When we *modify* nodes in the net, we must change the links in order not to create contradictions and thus ensure that inheritance is preserved.

3.   *Validation of semantic nets is difficult.* To validate the net we have to use complex scanning algorithms to check whether the net is circular, contains ambiguous information, or whether the net contains contradictory information.

4.   *Search time.* Since semantic nets are directed graphs, the search is linear and, therefore, very slow. If we use a semantic net in the implementation of an expert system, search time in the net will be a major hindrance to the performance of the expert system.

To overcome some of the difficulties described above, we introduce the concept of *frames* in the following section.


### 5.3.2 Frames

A frame is a data structure that combines within a single environment declarative and procedural knowledge with predefined internal relations [3]. The expert system selects the frame that is most applicable to the process of understanding the given current situation, and this frame in turn attempts to match itself to the data it discovers. If the frame is found to be inapplicable, control is transferred to a more appropriate frame.

An important feature of frames is that they can be arranged in a large frame-like structure that depicts the inter-relations among the constituent frames. The most basic relation between frames is the *parent - child relation* in which the parent frame represents a class of items whereas the set of child frames represents the class's subclasses, or specific members or instances of that class [28]. This feature is referred to as *inheritance* among frames.

Similarly to semantic nets, frames are also structured as directed graphs. The basic structure of a frame, depicted in Figure 5.5, consists of the following fields [3]:

1.   *Name* of the frame.

2.   *Parents* of the frame. This field indicates which frames (or ancestors) are linked to the current frame.

3.   *Slots.* A frame may contain no slots or a number of slots. Each slot contains a slot name, a *facet*[1], and a number of predicates or no predicates at all.

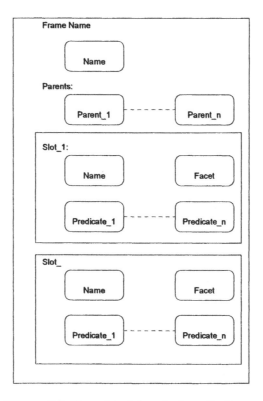

**Figure 5.5** Functional description of a frame

The feature of *inheritance* among frames is illustrated in Figure 5.6. In this figure, TOYOTA is a car which is a LAND VEHICLE that, based on inheritance, has four wheels and uses GAS to power its engine.

---

[1] Facets contain additional information related to the slot. One facet that a slot might have is RANGE which would contain the set of possible values for the slot. (A frame system with this feature would issue an error message if a value outside the range were to be inserted in the slot.) For example, the ON-SCHEDULE slot might have range = "Yes" or "No". Other common facets are DEFAULT VALUE, COMMENT, or the slot's VALUE itself.

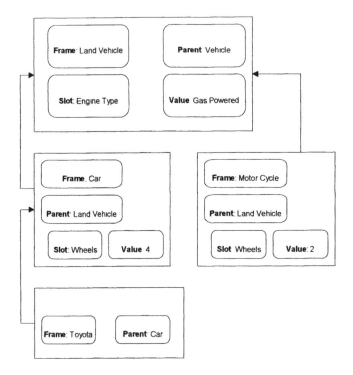

**Figure 5.6** Inheritance among frames

Frames are very powerful data structures for knowledge representation. They have, however, several drawbacks.

1.   Frames require large computer memory capacity for storage.

2.   Because frames are represented by directed graphs, the search is still slow although it is faster than the search in semantic nets.

3.   A very sophisticated inference engine is required to infer knowledge from frames and to associate correct properties to slots when inheritance occurs. For example, referring to Figure 5.6, if TOYOTA were to use electricity to power its engine, it should take precedence over the fact that its parent, LAND VEHICLE, has the property of being powered by gas.

### 5.3.3 Production Rules

*Production rules* representation is one of the most popular methods of knowledge representation in which knowledge is expressed by rules in the form of

*If P Then C*

where $P$ is the *premise* (or *antecedent*) of the rule, and $C$ is the *conclusion* (or *consequence*) of the rule.

The premise of the rule consists of clauses which are interconnected by operators such as AND, NOT, OR, NOR, NAND, Exclusive-Or (XOR), Equivalence, etc. The conclusion of the rule consists *only* of *true* statements in order to avoid ambiguity. Thus, the conclusion part in statements such as

*If a Then b OR c*

is not legitimate because such statement implies that either $b$ or $c$ may be true. Notice, however, that replacing the OR operator in the conclusion part of the rule by the AND operator would render the conclusion part unambiguous.

Therefore, the structure of the knowledge base in its most general form would consist of a list of rules such as:

$$\text{Rule\_1: } \textit{If } P_1 \textit{ Then } C_1$$

$$\text{Rule\_2: } \textit{If } P_2 \textit{ Then } C_2$$

.

.

$$\text{Rule\_i: } \textit{If } P_i \textit{ Then } C_i$$

.

.

$$\text{Rule\_n: } \textit{If } P_n \textit{ Then } C_n$$

Production rules formalism is a flexible mechanism that provides modularity and standardization of knowledge representation. Production rules can be used to represent several types of knowledge, as can be seen in the following examples [77].

- *Situation/action*: If it is raining, then carry an umbrella.

- *Premise/conclusion*: If it is snowing, then skiing is possible.

- *Sufficiency*: If it is drizzling, then the weather is gloomy.

- *Definition*: If it is raining, then water drops are falling from the sky.

Some of the important characteristics of knowledge representation using production rules are as follows [71].

- *Expressibility*. Rules can easily express basic symbol-processing acts such as actions, mathematical expressions, variables, and concepts.

- *Modularity.* Since inter-dependence between rules is quite limited, the order in which the rules are listed in the knowledge base is not important.

- *Modifiability.* Due to the limited interaction between rules, addition, deletion, or modification of rules has little effect on the other rules.

    Thus, when rules are added, deleted, or modified, they do not affect the structure of other rules, but affect only the relations among the rules.

- *Explainability.* The format of production rules is susceptible to natural languages, making the rules self-explanatory. Because the format of a rule is

    *If X Then Y*

    then to explain $Y$ we have to show $X$, which is a straightforward process.

- *Learning.* Since production rules have a standard format, learning new rules from existing ones can be done by finding correlations among the rules (data).

    We can also use supervised learning to change the structure of rules. This is explained in Chapter 8 where we describe how the expert system can learn about the grammar of the rules from examples provided by the user.

Production rules can be represented in a variety of ways which fall into three basic categories: *trees, bit matrices,* and *relational lists.* The tree representation consists of two types, rule-tree and clause-tree, whereas the bit-matrix representation consists of four types, rule bit-matrix, reduced rule bit-matrix, clause bit-matrix, and reduced clause bit-matrix. In the following paragraphs we discuss these various types of production rule representations.

```
FOR I:= 1 TO N DO BEGIN
    GET CONCLUSION OF RULE I
    FOR J:= 1 TO N DO BEGIN
        IF I≠J THEN BEGIN
            GET PREMISE OF RULE J
            IF Cᵢ∈Pⱼ THEN² ESTABLISH A LINK BETWEEN THE TWO RULES
        END
    END
END
```

**Algorithm 5.1** Procedure for constructing tree representation of a knowledge base

---

² $C_I$ is any clause in the conclusion of rule $I$, and $P_J$ is any clause in the premise of rule $J$.

### Tree Representation

The tree representation of a knowledge base exhibits the relations between the conclusions and the premises of the rules. The tree is a *directed graph* consisting of *nodes* that represent the rules and *links* that depict the relations between the conclusions and premises of the rules. We use circles to represent the nodes and arrows to represent links between them.

We construct the tree by traversing the knowledge base systematically, from the first rule to the last rule, to establish links between the conclusion part of the currently *checked* rule and the premise parts of all the other rules in the list. This procedure is summarized in Algorithm 5.1.

To illustrate the procedure for constructing the tree representation of a knowledge base, consider the knowledge base shown in Table 5.1 which consists of ten rules, R1 through R10.

**Table 5.1** Knowledge base example

| | |
|---|---|
| R1 | *If Q, Then X* |
| R2 | *If M, Then Y* |
| R3 | *If W AND X, Then G AND Z* |
| R4 | *If A AND B, Then C* |
| R5 | *If D OR Z, Then E* |
| R6 | *If C AND E, Then F* |
| R7 | *If X, Then A* |
| R8 | *If Y, Then B* |
| R9 | *If F, Then S* |
| R10 | *If G, Then R* |

Traversing the knowledge base from R1 to R10, we construct the tree representation in the following steps.

**Step 1**: *Check R1.* As we can see, rule R1 is linked to both R3 and R7 since $X$ is contained in the conclusion of R1 and in the premises of R3 and R7. The resulting tree representation is shown in Figure 5.7.

**Step 2**: *Check R2.* Rule R2 is linked to R8 because $Y$ is contained in the conclusion of R2 and in the premise of R8. Adding this information to the tree in Figure 5.7 yields the tree representation shown in Figure 5.8.

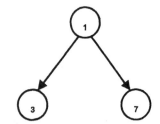

**Figure 5.7** Step 1

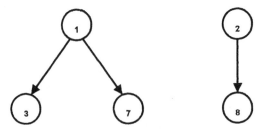

**Figure 5.8** Step 2

**Step 3**: *Check R3*. This rule is linked to R5 and R10 because both the conclusion of R3 and the premise of R5 contain Z, and both the conclusion of R3 and the premise of R10 contain G. Adding these links to Figure 5.8 results in the tree representation of Figure 5.9.

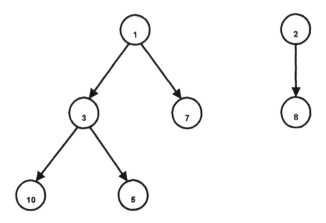

**Figure 5.9** Step 3

**Step 4**: *Check R4*. Rule R4 is linked to R6 since both the conclusion of R4 and the premise of R6 contain *C*. The resulting tree is depicted in Figure 5.10.

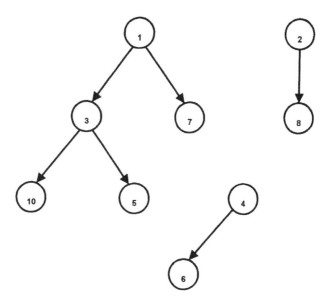

**Figure 5.10** Step 4

**Step 5**: *Check R5*. This rule is linked to R6 since *E* is contained in both the conclusion of R5 and the premise of R6. We add this link to the existing tree as shown in Figure 5.11.

**Step 6**: *Check R6*. This rule is linked to R9 via *F* in both the conclusion of R6 and the premise of R9.

**Step 7**: *Check R7*. Rule R7 is linked to R4 since *A* appears in the conclusion of R7 and in the premise of R4.

**Step 8**: *Check R8*. Since *B* appears in the conclusion of R8 and in the premise of R4, these two rules are linked.

**Step 9**: *Check R9*. This rule is not linked to any of the other rules.

**Step 10**: *Check R10*. This rule is not linked to any of the other rules.

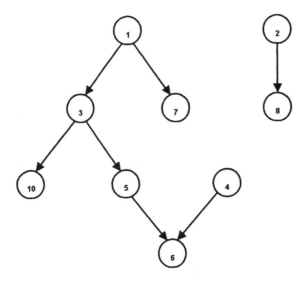

**Figure 5.11** Step 5

Adding the information resulting from Steps 6 to 10 to the tree in Figure 5.11, we get the *rule-tree representation* shown in Figure 5.12 for the knowledge base given in Table 5.1.

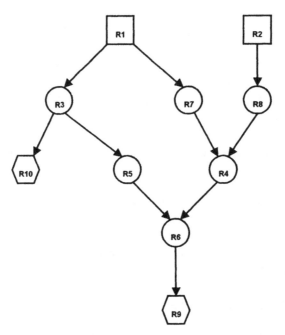

**Figure 5.12** Rule-tree representation

Note that in Figure 5.12 we have changed the graphical symbols of some of the nodes in order to distinguish between three types of rules:

1.  *root nodes* that correspond to *starting rules* are depicted by squares

2.  *terminal nodes* that correspond to *concluding rules* are depicted by hexagons

3.  *intermediate nodes* that correspond to *intermediate rules* are depicted by circles.

As we can see in Figure 5.12, nodes 1 and 2 are root nodes corresponding to the starting rules R1 and R2, nodes 9 and 10 are terminal nodes corresponding to the concluding rules R9 and R10, and the remaining nodes are intermediate nodes corresponding to the intermediate rules R3, R4, R5, R6, R7, and R8.

The problem with the rule-tree representation is that it does not show how clauses are related one to another. To alleviate this problem, we introduce another tree structure, referred to as the *clause-tree representation,* in which nodes represent clauses instead of rules.

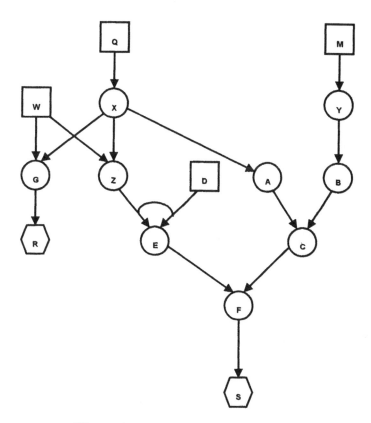

**Figure 5.13** Clause-tree representation

The clause-tree representation is constructed similarly to the rule-tree representation, and is shown in Figure 5.13 above for the knowledge base of Table 5.1. While we leave the actual derivation of the tree in Figure 5.13 as an exercise to the reader, let us consider briefly the interpretation of the graphical representation of the clause-tree.

In Figure 5.13, similarly to Figure 5.12, squares designate root nodes, hexagons designate terminal nodes, and circles designate intermediate nodes. Here, however, since the nodes correspond to clauses, root nodes correspond to clauses requiring user input, terminal nodes correspond to inferred conclusion clauses, and intermediate nodes correspond to intermediate premise/conclusion clauses.

Note that the clause-tree representation provides some additional information that is not provided by the rule-tree representation. In particular, the clause-tree representation depicts not *only* the relations between conclusion and premise clauses but also the *inter*-relations within premise clauses. To describe the inter-relation within premise clauses we use the following nomenclature: links connected together by arcs imply OR connectives; otherwise, the links imply AND connectives.

For example, since the premise of rule R5 is $D$ $OR$ $Z$, the links leading from nodes $D$ and $Z$ to node $E$ in Figure 5.13 are joined by an arc. By contrast, since the links leading from nodes $A$ and $B$ to node $C$ are not connected by an arc, the premise is understood to be $A$ $AND$ $B$ (refer to rule R4 in Table 5.1 for verification).

In general, the tree representation with its two variants has several very powerful characteristics.

1.  Tracing the tree can be accomplished very easily, enabling us to see how rules/clauses are related to one another.

2.  The inference process with the tree representation is fast. In particular, if we are looking for only one conclusion, we can search through one specific path and prune the rest of the tree.

3.  Explanation of the reasoning path is straightforward. We can trace the tree backward and show how we found a particular path.

However, using the tree structure may also be disadvantageous:

1.  The search is linear and, therefore, quite slow.

2.  It is difficult to validate the knowledge base. In particular, it is difficult to establish the presence of circular rules such as $R_i$ is linked to $R_j$, $R_j$ is linked to $R_k$, and $R_j$ is linked back to $R_i$.

3.  It is often impractical to use the tree representation if we are searching for multiple conclusions because we have to search the entire tree.

To overcome these drawbacks, we introduce next the *bit matrix* representation.

### Bit Matrix Representation

The bit-matrix knowledge representation is a data structure that is fast to trace, can generate multiple links, and is capable of validating the knowledge base for circular rules. To introduce the bit-matrix, notice that the tree representation of a knowledge base is actually a special case of a *finite state machine* in which the nodes are states that represent rules (or clauses) and the links depict the relations among the states.

We can associate the finite state machine with a matrix whose $(i, j)$ element represents the relation between the conclusion of rule $i$ and the premise of rule $j$. Stated formally, let **BM** (bit-matrix) be an $N{\times}N$ matrix, where $N$ is the number of rules in the knowledge base, and let $BM_{ij}$ denote the $(i, j)$ element of the matrix. Then:

$$BM_{ij} = \begin{cases} 1 & \textit{if the conclusion of rule i is linked to the premise of rule j} \\ 0 & \textit{otherwise} \end{cases}$$

Note that if $\sum_{j=1}^{n} BM_{ij} = 0$, then rule $i$ is a concluding rule (terminal node) in the tree representation of the knowledge base.

As we mentioned earlier, the bit-matrix representation can be of several types: *rule bit-matrix* (RBM), *reduced rule bit-matrix* (RRBM), *clause bit-matrix* (CBM), and *reduced clause bit-matrix* (RCBM). In the following paragraphs, we describe the structures of these representations and point out the advantages and disadvantages in using them.

**Rule bit-matrix:** The construction of the rule bit-matrix is similar to that of the rule-tree structure. We compare the conclusions of *each* rule to the premises of *every* rule. If a link is found, we set to 1 the corresponding element of the rule bit-matrix **RBM**.

To illustrate the construction of the rule bit-matrix, consider the knowledge base of Table 5.1 whose rule-tree representation is shown in Figure 5.12. There, we have established that R1 is linked to R3 and to R7. Hence, the $(1, 3)$ and $(1, 7)$ elements in the first row of the **RBM** are set to 1, whereas the remaining elements of that row are filled with 0's. In the second row of the **RBM**, only the $(2, 8)$ element is set to 1 because R2 is linked only to R8. Continuing in this manner, we get the **RBM** shown in Figure 5.14 that represents the example knowledge base.

Consider some of the advantages of using the rule bit-matrix representation.

1.   The rule bit-matrix can be processed in parallel, thus increasing the speed of the search. The order of the search speed for any particular link is $O(1)$.

2.   It is very easy to delete, add, or modify rules. To *delete* a rule, we simply remove the corresponding row and column. To *add* a rule, we add a row and a column to the matrix and check for links between the new rule and the

existing rules. To *modify* a rule, we first delete the rule and then add its modified version.

$$
\text{RBM} = \begin{bmatrix}
0 & 0 & 1 & 0 & 0 & 0 & 1 & 0 & 0 & 0 \\
0 & 0 & 0 & 0 & 0 & 0 & 0 & 1 & 0 & 0 \\
0 & 0 & 0 & 0 & 1 & 0 & 0 & 0 & 0 & 1 \\
0 & 0 & 0 & 0 & 0 & 1 & 0 & 0 & 0 & 0 \\
0 & 0 & 0 & 0 & 0 & 1 & 0 & 0 & 0 & 0 \\
0 & 0 & 0 & 0 & 0 & 0 & 0 & 0 & 1 & 0 \\
0 & 0 & 0 & 1 & 0 & 0 & 0 & 0 & 0 & 0 \\
0 & 0 & 0 & 1 & 0 & 0 & 0 & 0 & 0 & 0 \\
0 & 0 & 0 & 0 & 0 & 0 & 0 & 0 & 0 & 0 \\
0 & 0 & 0 & 0 & 0 & 0 & 0 & 0 & 0 & 0
\end{bmatrix}
$$

**Figure 5.14**  Rule bit-matrix representation

3.  We can use the rule bit-matrix to explain the reasoning path.

4.  The inference process can start anywhere in the decision tree.

5.  Using the rule bit-matrix, we can generate multiple conclusions (see Chapters 9 and 10).

6.  Validation of circular rules is straightforward as illustrated by the routine shown in Algorithm 5.2 below.

Nevertheless, the rule bit-matrix data structure has two drawbacks.

1.  The rule bit-matrix does not provide information about the relations among the clauses in the knowledge base (similarly to the problem we had with the rule-tree representation).

2.  The rule bit-matrix requires considerable computer memory space for storage, however, most of it is wasted because the matrix is sparse.

To circumvent the first problem, we introduce the clause bit-matrix and the reduced clause bit-matrix in the following paragraphs. To deal with the second problem, we can do one of two things.

1.  We can transform the matrix into a two-dimensional linked list. This will save computer memory space but will make the search linear, that is, increase the search time.

2.  We can use the reduced rule bit-matrix introduced in the next paragraph. This will save some computer memory space and will not increase the search time by much.

```
T:= RBM; {T denote some temporary matrix}
FOR I:= 1 TO N DO
    X:=0;
    {Count the number of ones on the diagonal and store result in X}
    FOR J:=1 to N DO X:= X+ T[J,J];
    {If X>0 then there is a case where a rule is linked to itself}
    If X>0 THEN THE MATRIX IS NOT VALID; EXIT;
    X:=0;
    {Count the number of ones in T and store result in X}
    FOR J:=1 TO N DO
        FOR K:=1 TO N DO
            X:=X+T[J,K];
    {If X=0 then the matrix is empty and thus it is valid; no circularity}
    IF X=0 THEN THE MATRIX IS VALID; EXIT;
    T:=T*RBM
END;
{Compute again the value of T}
X:=0;
FOR I:=1 TO N DO
    FOR J:=1 TO N DO
        X:= X+T[I,J];
{Determine if the matrix is valid}
IF X=0 THEN THE MATRIX IS VALID
    ELSE IT IS NOT VALID
```

**Algorithm 5.2** Validation of circular rules

**Reduced rule bit-matrix:** The reduced rule bit-matrix was suggested in order to reduce the computer memory space required to store the rule bit-matrix without increasing the search time. We discuss these two issues later in this section.

The reduced rule bit-matrix, **RRBM**, is derived from the rule bit-matrix, **RBM**, by removing from the **RBM** rows and columns that contain only zeros. In other words, we remove all the *starting rules* and the *concluding rules* from the **RBM**. To illustrate this process, consider the knowledge base of Table 5.1, whose rule-tree representation is shown in Figure 5.12, for which we derived the rule bit-matrix in Figure 5.14.

Since R1 and R2 are starting rules, whereas R9 and R10 are concluding rules, we can remove their corresponding columns (the first two columns in Figure 5.14) and their corresponding rows (the last two rows in Figure 5.14), respectively, to obtain the reduced rule bit-matrix depicted in Figure 5.15.

$$\mathbf{RRBM} = \begin{bmatrix} 1 & 0 & 0 & 0 & 1 & 0 & 0 & 0 \\ 0 & 0 & 0 & 0 & 0 & 1 & 0 & 0 \\ 0 & 0 & 1 & 0 & 0 & 0 & 0 & 1 \\ 0 & 0 & 0 & 1 & 0 & 0 & 0 & 0 \\ 0 & 0 & 0 & 1 & 0 & 0 & 0 & 0 \\ 0 & 0 & 0 & 0 & 0 & 0 & 1 & 0 \\ 0 & 1 & 0 & 0 & 0 & 0 & 0 & 0 \\ 0 & 1 & 0 & 0 & 0 & 0 & 0 & 0 \end{bmatrix}$$

**Figure 5.15** Reduced rule bit-matrix representation

Notice, however, that in the process of deleting rows and columns from the **RBM** to derive the **RRBM**, we lose the pointers that indicate which row and column correspond to which rule. To remedy this situation, we augment the **RRBM** with two *index vectors*, referred to as column and row headers, which indicate how the rows and columns are related to the corresponding rules. This is shown in Figure 5.16 which depicts the **RRBM** of Figure 5.15 in its augmented form. Both index vectors designate rule numbers; the column header pertains to the premises of the rules and the row header pertains to the conclusions of the rules.

|   | 3 | 4 | 5 | 6 | 7 | 8 | 9 | 10 |
|---|---|---|---|---|---|---|---|---|
| 1 | 1 | 0 | 0 | 0 | 1 | 0 | 0 | 0 |
| 2 | 0 | 0 | 0 | 0 | 0 | 1 | 0 | 0 |
| 3 | 0 | 0 | 1 | 0 | 0 | 0 | 0 | 1 |
| 4 | 0 | 0 | 0 | 1 | 0 | 0 | 0 | 0 |
| 5 | 0 | 0 | 0 | 1 | 0 | 0 | 0 | 0 |
| 6 | 0 | 0 | 0 | 0 | 0 | 0 | 1 | 0 |
| 7 | 0 | 1 | 0 | 0 | 0 | 0 | 0 | 0 |
| 8 | 0 | 1 | 0 | 0 | 0 | 0 | 0 | 0 |

**Figure 5.16** Augmented reduced rule bit-matrix

Let us now discuss how using the **RRBM** reduces the computer memory space required to store the **RBM** without increasing the search time. Consider first the issue of search time. Assume that the **RBM** and **RRBM** are $N \times N$ and $M \times K$ matrices, respectively, where $M, K < N$. Notice that a valid knowledge base *must* always contain at least one *starting rule* and one *concluding rule* and, therefore, $N$ must be greater than $M$ and $K$.

Although we add two index vectors to the **RRBM**, the search time is still very fast because we can use binary search to search rules in the vectors and then go to the corresponding entry in the matrix. Thus, the search time is $O(lnN + lnM + 1)$ in the worst case. The nice thing about the reduced rule bit-matrix data structure is that if we search the column index vector and do not find a rule, then it must be a concluding rule, and if we cannot find a rule in the row index vector, then it is a starting rule.

The second issue pertains to the computer storage requirements. We will show that although we add two index vectors to the **RRBM**, its size is generally still smaller than that of the **RBM** due to the removal of zero rows and columns. To see this, note that the size of the augmented **RRBM** is $MK + M + K$, $M, K \leq N$, where $M$ and $K$ are the dimensions of the **RRBM**. Assuming that $M > K$, we can add $M - K$ columns to the **RRBM** so that it would be an $M \times M$ matrix[3]. If we now append the two index vectors, then the size of the augmented **RRBM** becomes $2M + M^2$.

Hence, since $N > M$, we want to show that $N^2 > 2M + M^2$. To verify this inequality, let $M = N - D$ and rewrite the inequality as:

$$N^2 > 2(N - D) + (N - D)^2$$

or as:

$$N^2 > N^2 - 2DN + 2N - 2D + D^2$$

Rearranging terms, we get the following quadratic inequality in $D$,

$$-D^2 + 2(N + 1)D - 2N > 0$$

whose solutions are

$$D_1 = N + 1 + \sqrt{N^2 + 1}$$

and

$$D_2 = N + 1 - \sqrt{N^2 + 1}$$

Substituting these solutions into $M = N - D$, yields:

$$M_1 = -1 - \sqrt{N^2 + 1} < 0$$

---

[3] This is the worst possible case. If we show that the computer memory space requirement of the $M \times M$ matrix is still less than that required by the **RBM**, then clearly the **RRBM** itself requires an even smaller memory space.

and

$$M_2 = -1 + \sqrt{N^2 + 1} > 0 \quad \text{(unless } N = 0\text{)}$$

Consequently, $M_2$ is the only relevant solution that satisfies the original inequality $N^2 > 2M + M^2$, and we can conclude that the **RRBM** needs less computer memory for the storage than does the **RBM**.

Note that the solution $M_2$ implies that we will save space even if we reduce the **RBM** by exactly one row and one column. Since we know that knowledge bases usually have more than one starting rule and one concluding rule, we can conclude that the **RRBM** definitely needs less computer memory than the **RBM**.

**Clause bit-matrix:** The clause bit-matrix is introduced in order to display the relations among clauses in the knowledge base. We construct the clause bit-matrix, **CBM**, as follows:

1.  We assign a unique *identification number* (ID) to each clause in the premises of the rules in the knowledge base.

    For example, using our knowledge base of Table 5.1, we assign *ID(5,2)* to the clause $Z$ in the premise of R5 to indicate that $Z$ is the second clause in the premise of R5.

2.  We assign a unique *identification number* (ID) to each clause in the conclusions of the rules in the knowledge base.

    For example, we assign *ID(3,1)* to the clause $G$ in the conclusion of R3 to indicate that $G$ is the first clause in the conclusion of rule 3.

3.  We enter the elements of the **CBM** by searching for links between the clauses similarly to the construction of the clause-tree.

The construction procedure of the clause bit-matrix is illustrated in Figure 5.17, which shows the **CBM** for the knowledge base of Table 5.1. As we can see, the construction procedure of the **CBM** results in the addition of two 2-dimensional *index vectors* to the matrix.

Similarly to the index vectors associated with the reduced rule bit-matrix, the 2-dimensional row header pertains to the conclusions of the rules and the 2-dimensional column header pertains to the premises of the rules. The first (top-most) column index vector and the first (left-side) row index vector designate rule numbers whereas the second column and row index vectors designate clause numbers. Thus, for example, the entry [2 1] of the 2-dimensional row header points to the conclusion of rule 2 clause 1, and the entry $\begin{bmatrix} 2 \\ 1 \end{bmatrix}$ of the 2-dimensional column header points to the premise of rule 2 clause 1.

Notice that the **CBM** requires more memory space for storage than the **RBM** and that the search is slower. We must search each vector linearly so that the order of the search is $O(2N+1)$. We cannot improve the search time but we can reduce the size of the **CBM** by using the *reduced clause bit-matrix* described in the next paragraph.

| | | 1 | 2 | 3 | 3 | 4 | 4 | 5 | 5 | 6 | 6 | 7 | 8 | 9 | 10 |
| --- | --- | --- | --- | --- | --- | --- | --- | --- | --- | --- | --- | --- | --- | --- | --- |
| | | 1 | 1 | 1 | 2 | 1 | 2 | 1 | 2 | 1 | 2 | 1 | 1 | 1 | 1 |
| 1 | 1 | 0 | 0 | 0 | 1 | 0 | 0 | 0 | 0 | 0 | 0 | 1 | 0 | 0 | 0 |
| 2 | 1 | 0 | 0 | 0 | 0 | 0 | 0 | 0 | 0 | 0 | 0 | 0 | 1 | 0 | 0 |
| 3 | 1 | 0 | 0 | 0 | 0 | 0 | 0 | 0 | 0 | 0 | 0 | 0 | 0 | 0 | 1 |
| 3 | 2 | 0 | 0 | 0 | 0 | 0 | 0 | 0 | 1 | 0 | 0 | 0 | 0 | 0 | 0 |
| 4 | 1 | 0 | 0 | 0 | 0 | 0 | 0 | 0 | 0 | 1 | 0 | 0 | 0 | 0 | 0 |
| 5 | 1 | 0 | 0 | 0 | 0 | 0 | 0 | 0 | 0 | 0 | 1 | 0 | 0 | 0 | 0 |
| 6 | 1 | 0 | 0 | 0 | 0 | 0 | 0 | 0 | 0 | 0 | 0 | 0 | 0 | 1 | 0 |
| 7 | 1 | 0 | 0 | 0 | 0 | 1 | 0 | 0 | 0 | 0 | 0 | 0 | 0 | 0 | 0 |
| 8 | 1 | 0 | 0 | 0 | 0 | 0 | 1 | 0 | 0 | 0 | 0 | 0 | 0 | 0 | 0 |
| 9 | 1 | 0 | 0 | 0 | 0 | 0 | 0 | 0 | 0 | 0 | 0 | 0 | 0 | 0 | 0 |
| 10 | 1 | 0 | 0 | 0 | 0 | 0 | 0 | 0 | 0 | 0 | 0 | 0 | 0 | 0 | 0 |

**Figure 5.17** Clause bit-matrix representation

**Reduced clause bit-matrix:** To reduce the size of the **CBM**, we remove from it all the rows and columns that contain zeros. The resulting matrix is called the reduced clause bit-matrix. Figure 5.18 shows the reduced clause bit-matrix, **RCBM**, for our knowledge base of Table 5.1, derived from the **CBM** in Figure 5.17. (Refer to the previous section pertaining to the clause bit-matrix for explanation regarding the two 2-dimensional *index vectors* shown in Figure 5.18.)

As we can see, while the **RCBM** reduces the memory space required for storage, it is still quite large. Furthermore, since the two 2-dimensional index vectors must be searched linearly, the search time is of the order $O(2N+1)$, similarly to that of the **CBM**.

|   |   | 3 | 4 | 4 | 5 | 6 | 6 | 7 | 8 | 9 | 10 |
|---|---|---|---|---|---|---|---|---|---|---|----|
|   |   | 2 | 1 | 2 | 2 | 1 | 2 | 1 | 1 | 1 | 1  |
| 1 | 1 | *1* | *0* | *0* | *0* | *0* | *0* | *1* | *0* | *0* | *0* |
| 2 | 1 | *0* | *0* | *0* | *0* | *0* | *0* | *0* | *1* | *0* | *0* |
| 3 | 1 | *0* | *0* | *0* | *0* | *0* | *0* | *0* | *0* | *0* | *1* |
| 3 | 2 | *0* | *0* | *0* | *1* | *0* | *0* | *0* | *0* | *0* | *0* |
| 4 | 1 | *0* | *0* | *0* | *0* | *1* | *0* | *0* | *0* | *0* | *0* |
| 5 | 1 | *0* | *0* | *0* | *0* | *0* | *1* | *0* | *0* | *0* | *0* |
| 6 | 1 | *0* | *0* | *0* | *0* | *0* | *0* | *0* | *0* | *1* | *0* |
| 7 | 1 | *0* | *1* | *0* | *0* | *0* | *0* | *0* | *0* | *0* | *0* |
| 8 | 1 | *0* | *0* | *1* | *0* | *0* | *0* | *0* | *0* | *0* | *0* |

**Figure 5.18** Reduced clause bit-matrix representation

### *Relational List Representation*

We want a knowledge representation that is easy to build and modify, that is fast to search, and that will let us produce multiple conclusions. It turns out that, with all the advantages and disadvantages of using bit matrices, the best way to represent knowledge is via a special list, called the *relational list*, that depicts the relations among clauses in the knowledge base.

The relational list (R-list) is a simple data structure whose construction is straightforward. It can be modified easily, allows fast searching, and it enables the inference process to generate multiple conclusions. However, the main advantage of the R-list is that it is most amenable to the inclusion of *fuzzy* information about the relations between clauses in the knowledge base in a straightforward manner.

Therefore, the R-list is the preferred data structure for knowledge representation in fuzzy expert systems such as our FEST, and will be used extensively throughout the remainder of this book. It provides us with all the necessary information that is contained in the **CBM** or the **RCBM**, yet it is faster to search than these two matrices.

The R-list is a 6-tuple list in which the first two columns indicate the *identification numbers* (ID) of the conclusion clauses, the next two columns represent the IDs of the premise clauses, and the last two columns designate respectively the *matching factor* and the *membership grade* between the two clauses. As an example, Figure 5.19 shows the R-list representation of the knowledge base of Table 5.1.

Recall that we have already introduced the notion of the ID of the premise and conclusion clauses in the discussion of the clause bit-matrix, and introduced the concept of membership grade in Chapter 3. We defer the discussion of the matching factor and the types of fuzzy information that may affect the last two columns in the R-list to Chapters 6 and 7.

| Conclusion Clause | | Premise Clause | | Matching Factor | Membership Grade |
|---|---|---|---|---|---|
| Rule # | Clause # | Rule # | Clause # | | |
| 1 | 1 | 3 | 2 | 1 | –2 |
| 1 | 1 | 7 | 1 | 1 | –2 |
| 2 | 1 | 8 | 1 | 1 | –2 |
| 3 | 1 | 10 | 1 | 1 | –2 |
| 3 | 2 | 5 | 2 | 1 | –2 |
| 4 | 1 | 6 | 1 | 1 | –2 |
| 5 | 1 | 6 | 2 | 1 | –2 |
| 6 | 1 | 9 | 1 | 1 | –2 |
| 7 | 1 | 4 | 1 | 1 | –2 |
| 8 | 1 | 4 | 2 | 1 | –2 |

**Figure 5.19** Relational list representation

## 5.4 Knowledge Generation

When the knowledge engineer completes the task of acquiring knowledge from the expert(s), he/she has to decide, based on the knowledge representation schemes described in Section 5.3, on the best data structure for representing the knowledge within the expert system. Having made this decision, the *knowledge generation* process can begin.

To complete our discussion of the process of embedding knowledge within the expert system, we outline in this section two approaches for generating a knowledge base. The second of these approaches will be discussed further in Chapter 8. These two approaches are referred to as *user input* and *autonomous input*.

1.  *User input.* We can use a text editor to enter the knowledge to the expert system. The expert system can then parse the knowledge, check for syntax problems, and create its internal structure. This is a simple process but is time consuming and is prone to errors.

2.  *Autonomous input.* We can use a specially-constructed tool that accepts *raw* knowledge and converts it autonomously into a valid knowledge base [103, 104, 105]. The raw knowledge is usually in text form and can be imported to the expert system. In FEST, this is done using the *import* command (see Chapter 8). When the *import* command is executed, FEST parses the input knowledge base and places its components in the proper data structures.

# 6 IMPRECISION AND FUZZY LOGIC

It is not necessary to represent one's state of certainty in order to solve problems under uncertainty. Often, uncertainty succumbs to solving a problem by following an appropriately designed control strategy that specifies what the problem solver should do next. By exploiting the properties of an uncertain domain in the design of the control strategy, we can reduce the effects of uncertainty.

As an illustration, consider a possible control strategy for solving a jigsaw puzzle. If we let the fuzzy variable $A$ represent the linguistic term *anything*, then we can work on $A$ next, or we can attempt to build the frame of the puzzle first, namely, we can exploit the fact that frame components have at least one straight edge. Having built the frame, we can again work on $A$ next, or we can search for puzzle components that extend the frame inwards, namely, exploit the property that puzzle components fit together.

Usually, the strategy of building the frame first and working inwards solves the jigsaw puzzle faster than the *do anything first* strategy. Nevertheless, in both cases there is uncertainty about the placement of any given puzzle component, but with a smart control strategy we can *grade* this uncertainty: edge components are the least uncertain and should be worked in first, and then, any component that looks as if it might extend the frame is less uncertain than any other component whose placement is completely unconstrained.

The control strategy approach to uncertainty is often used when the goal is to interpret noisy but converging evidence. For example, line-finding algorithms for image understanding must contend with noisy image data but, sometimes, the partially-understood image can be used as a guide to further processing the image.

Human reasoning and the communication of knowledge and ideas are mostly done using *natural language*. Natural language has greater flexibility by comparison to strict mathematical formulations, particularly in areas where quantification is too restrictive.

Another important advantage of utilizing natural language is the ability to understand an expert's views on the solutions to a given problem, in particular when the problem is so complex that it cannot be formulated mathematically or even when its details are unknown. In addition, in most cases, it is easier to explain or understand things in natural language terms. For example, using natural language to teach another person how to park a car is by far easier and more efficient than attempting to express this activity in terms of complex differential equations.

Any computer program decides which data to handle and which calculations to perform, especially when we view the computer as a logician rather than as a calculator. All computer programs embody human knowledge about the way the world is, about some human goals, and about the way to achieve those goals.

The word *reasoning*, used in the context of computer programs, indicates that the program represents attempts to mimic as closely as possible the way human experts themselves use their own knowledge to make logically sound conclusions. In some cases, human experts express their knowledge via vague descriptions or buzz words and have a *feeling* of how to solve the problem.

But how do we represent buzz words and feelings? How do we represent decisions that are based on real world situations? How can we represent a statement such as *"If Tim is very tall Then he must be more or less heavy?"*

Imprecision and vagueness are built into natural language and allow for its versatility and potential for development. In this respect, natural language can be compared to the human hand which despite its adaptability to the most diverse tasks is still inaccurate. We build artificial hands, tools for particular purposes, which are much more accurate than the human hand. But how is this accuracy possible? Through the very stiffness and inflexibility of parts the artificial hand, the lack of which makes the human hand so dexterous. In this respect, natural language is similar to the human hand.

What we need, therefore, is a symbolic language that has a strict logical form from which content (meaning) cannot escape. Boolean logic is inappropriate because of its *two-valued* structure which is inapplicable to most real-life situations. Fuzzy logic, on the other hand, provides us with the tools to handle situations which embody fuzziness and vagueness.

Hence, a particular advantage of a *fuzzy expert system* is its ability to operate in uncertain environments or with fuzzy data.

# 6.1 Overview Of Imprecision

Decision making is crucial in virtually all human activities. The procedures used by humans to manipulate data are often not precisely specified. However, this is not necessarily due to the intrinsic imprecision of the natural language we use, nor is it due to our inability to put things into words. We are certainly able to use natural language to express things in a precise way most of the time.

Often, procedures to manipulate data are not precisely specified because we do not have the means to perform precise measurements, or because it may be impossible to do so, or simply because it may be unnecessary and too expensive. In other cases, precision is not necessarily meaningful, especially in human affairs. For example, the required profile of a candidate to a position is usually specified linguistically although the elements of this profile often can be more or less evaluated or graded in a numerical way. While we may assign arbitrary values to what is only roughly specified, or we may refuse to consider anything that is imprecise, it seems more natural and useful to accept imprecise data or procedures and deal with them as such because imprecision, or fuzziness, is often an unavoidable feature in human reasoning systems.

Consider the following two examples [73]. The first is concerned with establishing an entrance criterion for admitting students into some study program. The criterion is based on the weighted mean of the grades obtained by the student in three examinations, say mathematics, English, and French literature. The grades belong to a set of six levels *A, B, C, D, E,* and *F*, which may be linguistically interpreted as *very good, good, rather good, rather bad, bad, very bad*, respectively. (This kind of grading system is actually used in French schools.) The question is, what procedure should we use that will enable us to select a student who is *at least good in mathematics and at least rather good in French literature or English*?

The second example concerns a sentence such as: *go about 300 m due North where you will see a narrow street; take this street and almost immediately you will see the bank*. Note that in this example, the success of the procedure is guaranteed (if backtracking is allowed) because there exists a landmark (the bank) which enables one to control (in the sense of automatics) the position.

Many mathematical models have been designed to answer the above questions, both from the descriptive and prescriptive perspective. Strong analytical results and efficient numerical procedures have appeared. Unfortunately, their use in practice has often encountered difficulties. Since it is usually a human decision-maker who should act on the obtained results, the model should be consistent with human value systems, perceptions, etc., rather than with mathematical formalism and niceties. However, human value systems and perceptions are usually imprecise or vague (fuzzy, for short) and cannot be directly captured by the conventional *precise* mathematics.

Continuing the quest for making the decision models more consistent with how people perceive the very essence of the situations modeled, it has been argued that we should reflect in our models *commonsense* which people are explicitly or implicitly using. When we say *winter days are cold*, we implicitly involve a linguistic quantifier such as *most*. Thus, what we really mean is that *most winter days are cold*. Indeed, linguistic quantifiers play a crucial role in the representation of commonsense knowledge, and they can be manipulated via fuzzy logic.

Commonsense knowledge is an apparatus for representing and manipulating propositions that implicitly involve quantifiers. By introducing them into decision-making models, we obtain formulations that reflect better the practical human perception of both the essence of the modeled situation and what the solutions should mean, and guarantee a better acceptance of the modeling results by human decision makers. The presented approach is therefore not only analytically interesting but also practically relevant.

According to Lotfi Zadeh [109]:

> "Clearly the *class of real numbers which are much greater than one*, or the *class of beautiful women*, or the *class of tall men* do not constitute classes or sets in the usual mathematical sense of these terms. Yet, the fact remains that such imprecisely defined *classes* play an important role in human thinking, particularly in the domains of expert systems, pattern recognition, communication of information, and abstraction."

Zadeh also notes that certain complex activities involving human control, such as properly mixing ingredients in a chemical process or parking a car, cannot be *precisely* modeled. Yet, fuzzy set theory was quickly applied to various areas of research, notably decision theory [107] and artificial intelligence [29].

Recently, there has been considerable interest on the part of linguists and computer scientists in problems such as the role of vagueness in language and the quantification of meaning. Much of this interest has been the result of the development of fuzzy set theory which is a generalization of the two-valued set theory. A major feature of fuzzy set theory is that a quantitatively specified system can contain linguistic variables in addition to numeric variables. These linguistic variables can be manipulated and operated upon in much the same way as numeric variables in non-fuzzy systems. This new way of dealing with complex systems appears quite promising in terms of specifying complex behavioural processes such as the measurement of word meaning or the description of reasoning processes in everyday situations.

The knowledge base of an expert system is a repository of human knowledge. Since much of human knowledge is imprecise in nature, the knowledge base usually consists of a collection of rules and facts most of which are neither totally certain nor totally consistent, unless the knowledge engineer specifically wants them so. The uncertainty of information in the knowledge base induces some uncertainty in the validity of the drawn conclusions. Hence, to serve a useful purpose, the answer to a question must be associated, explicitly or at least implicitly, with an assessment of its reliability. For this reason, a basic issue in the design of expert systems is how to equip them with the computational ability of analyzing the transmission of uncertainty from the premises to the conclusions of the rules, and of associating the conclusion with what is commonly called a *certainty factor*.

In various expert systems, such as *MYCIN* [88] and *PROSPECTOR* [18], the computation of certainty factors is carried out through a combination of methods which are based on two-valued logic and probability theory. However, it is recognized that such methods have serious shortcomings and, for the most part, are difficult to rationalize. In particular, the usual assumption that the certainty factor of the conclusion is a function of the certainty factors associated with the premises is, in general, invalid. By contrast, however, this assumption regains its validity if the certainty factors are represented as fuzzy rather than crisp numbers.

The point of view articulated here is that conventional approaches to the management of uncertainty in expert systems are intrinsically inadequate because they fail to come to grips with the fact that much of the uncertainty in such systems is possibilistic rather than probabilistic in nature. As an alternative, the use of a computational framework based on fuzzy logic is suggested to deal with both possibilistic and probabilistic uncertainty within a single conceptual system. In this system, test-score semantics form the basis for the representation of knowledge, while the inferential component of fuzzy logic is employed to deduce answers to questions and, when necessary, associate each answer with a probability which is represented as a fuzzy quantifier [116].

Fuzzy logic implies that, given the fuzzy rule:

$$\alpha_F \xrightarrow{\quad F \quad} \beta_F$$

and the data $\alpha_F^*$ (where the * means that the two propositions are similar but not identical), we can conclude that some $\beta_F^*$ is true to some degree. Each of the propositions can consist of one or more clauses separated by the logical operator AND, OR and NOT which are interpreted as *min*, *max*, and *negation* (see Chapter 3). We will discuss the algorithm for determining the degree of similarity between two proposition in Chapter 7.

Using fuzzy logic in the framework of managing uncertainty in expert systems makes it possible to consider a number of issues which cannot be dealt with effectively or correctly by conventional techniques. The more important of these issues are the following.

1. *Fuzziness of antecedents and/or consequents* in rules of the form,

   *If X is A Then Y is B*

   *If X is A Then Y is B with CF = α*

   where the antecedent *X is A* and the consequent *Y is B* are fuzzy propositions, and $\alpha$ is the value of the certainty factor (*CF*). For example, in the rule

*If X is small Then Y is large with CF = 0.8*

the antecedent *X is small* and the consequent *Y is large* are fuzzy propositions because the denotations of the predicates *small* and *large* are the fuzzy subsets SMALL and LARGE.

2.  *Partial matching between the antecedent of a rule and a fact supplied by the user.* There may be cases in an expert system in which a fact such as

$$X \text{ is } A^*$$

does not match exactly the antecedent of any rule of the form

*If X is A Then Y is B with CF = $\alpha$*

Conventional rule-based systems usually avoid this issue, or treat it in an ad hoc manner, because partial matching does not lend itself to analysis within the confines of two-valued logic. By contrast, the gradation of truth and membership in fuzzy logic provides a natural way of dealing with partial matching through the use of the compositional rule of inference and interpolation [85].

3.  *Fuzzy quantifiers in the antecedent and/or the consequent of a rule.* In many cases, the antecedent and/or the consequent of a rule contain implicit or explicit fuzzy quantifiers such as *most, many, usually,* as well as compound fuzzy terms such as *not very low.* Examples of the fuzzy terms and compound fuzzy terms of natural language are illustrated in Tables 6.1 and 6.2.

**Table 6.1** Examples of fuzzy terms

| |
|---|
| *low* |
| *medium* |
| *high* |
| *very* |
| *more or less* |
| *several* |
| *few* |
| *many* |
| *most* |
| *approximately* |

**Table 6.2** Examples of compound fuzzy terms

> *not very low*
>
> *not more or less low*
>
> *medium to sort of high*
>
> *higher than slightly low*
>
> *low to sort of medium*
>
> *most high*

Consider the statement "*students are young*". It can be interpreted as the proposition "*most of the students are young*" which, in turn, may be expressed as the rule (the conditional proposition):

*If x is a student Then it is likely that x is young*

In this case, the fuzzy probability *likely* has the same denotation, expressed as a fuzzy subset of the unit interval, as the fuzzy quantifier *most*.

As was already mentioned, fuzzy logic provides a natural framework for the management of uncertainty in expert systems because, in contrast to the traditional logic systems, it provides a systematic way for representing and inferring from imprecise rather than precise knowledge. In fact, in fuzzy sets everything is allowed to be, but need not be, a matter of degree. The greater expressive power of fuzzy logic derives from the fact that it contains as special cases the traditional two-valued logic as well as multi-valued logic.

The main features of fuzzy sets which are relevant to the management of uncertainty in the expert systems are the following.

1.  In a two-valued set system, a proposition *p* is either true or false. In a multi-valued set system, a proposition may be true, or can have an intermediate truth-value which may be an element of the finite or infinite truth-value set T. In fuzzy sets, the truth values are allowed to range over the fuzzy subsets of T. For example, if T is the unit interval, then a truth-value in fuzzy sets, such as *very true*, may be interpreted as a fuzzy subset of the unit interval which defines the possibility distribution associated with the truth-value in question. In this sense, a fuzzy truth-value may be viewed as an imprecise characterization of an intermediate truth-value.

2.  The predicates in a two-valued set system are constrained to be crisp in the sense that the denotation of a predicate must be a non-fuzzy subset of the universe of discourse. In fuzzy-sets, the predicates may be crisp such as

*mortal, even, father of,* or fuzzy such as *ill, tired, large, tall, much heavier, friend of.*

3.    Two-valued logic, as well as multi-valued logic, allows only two quantifiers: *all* and *some.* By contrast, fuzzy logic allows, in addition, the use of fuzzy quantifiers exemplified by *most, several, much, few of, occasionally, frequently,* etc. Such quantifiers may be interpreted as fuzzy numbers that provide an imprecise characterization of the cardinality of one or more fuzzy or non-fuzzy sets. In this perspective, a fuzzy quantifier may be used to represent the meaning of propositions containing fuzzy probabilities and, thereby, makes it possible to manipulate probabilities within fuzzy sets.

Fuzzy set theory provides a method for representing the meaning of both non-fuzzy and fuzzy predicate-modifiers such as *not, very, more or less, extremely, slightly, a little.* In turn, this leads to a system for computing with linguistic variables [72, 112], namely, variables whose values are words or sentences in a natural or synthetic language. For example, *age* is a linguistic variable with values such as *very young, young, not very old, old, very old,* where each value is interpreted as possibility distribution over the real line.

## 6.2  Fuzziness In Expert Systems

Uncertainty management is one of the most important characteristics of an expert system [35, 56, 71, 121]. Proper handling of fuzzy knowledge and data brings any expert system one step closer to emulating experts in their decision-making process [46, 47, 58].

There are several types of fuzziness associated with any rule-based expert system.

• *Confidence in a given rule.* Given the rule *If P Then C,* we ask: How true is this rule, that is, what confidence do we have in it, and how it can contribute to the solution of the problem? This is called *rule certainty* and can be viewed as another representation of fuzzy probability. We can say that rule $R_i$ is *usually* true but not always. Hence, the numerical value of the rule certainty replaces the linguistic values *usually, in most cases,* etc.

Another question has to do with the relation between the premise $P$ and the conclusion $C$ of the rule. Given that the premise has some truth, what will be the truth of the conclusion? This is called the *conclusion certainty.* For example, the rule *If it is cold Then wear a coat* gives rise to the question: Given that it is cold, how sure are we that wearing a coat will make us more comfortable?

• *Rule priority.* Rule priority is used to rank the rules in the order in which they will be activated. Basically, this parameter enables us to take into consideration the importance of a rule in solving (or participating in solving) the problem.

- *Confidence in the given data.* When the user provides the necessary data to the expert system, we have to take into account the truth of that data. Often, the user provides data in which he/she does not have complete confidence. For example, the user may say "I think that the length of the fibre is 7 inches, but I'm not sure". In this case, we have to assign some grade of confidence to the given data. This is called *data certainty*.

- *Fuzziness in data and knowledge description.* In many cases, the knowledge and/or the data are described in fuzzy terms. For example, *John is more or less old*, or *the range of the target is between 20 and 24 yards*. We have to develop a model that will enable us to handle these fuzzy descriptions.

- *Fuzzy matching.* When the data provided to the expert system do not match exactly the knowledge base, we have to apply a matching procedure to evaluate the similarity between the incoming data and the knowledge base.

We can divide the above types of fuzziness into three different classes according to where they can be found.

1. Rule certainty, conclusion certainty, rule priority, and knowledge description are associated with the knowledge base.

2. Data certainty and data description can be found in the data provided by the user (or by any other means of communication).

3. Fuzzy matching is applied when the relational list (see Chapter 5) is generated, and when the inference engine matches the knowledge against the data.

Because the incorporation of the various types of fuzziness slows the expert system's execution time, the need for a preprocessing phase becomes apparent. In this phase, we can compute the overall confidence in the rule and create links among the rules in the knowledge base. Then, in the execution phase, we have to parse the data, match it with the knowledge base, and compute the certainty of the conclusions. In Chapter 7 we describe the preprocessing procedures.

# 7 KNOWLEDGE PROCESSING

As was indicated in the previous chapter, knowledge processing is a very important stage in the design and operation of fuzzy expert systems (or any other type of expert system for that matter). Properly handled, knowledge processing ensures fast and proper execution of the inferencing process.

This chapter is devoted to the three steps that comprise the knowledge processing stage:

1. compiling subjective knowledge

2. parsing the knowledge base

3. creating linkages among the rules in the knowledge base and storing them in the relational list.

## 7.1 Compiling Subjective Knowledge

Each rule in the knowledge base is associated with three confidence parameters: the *rule confidence* (*RC*), *conclusion confidence* (*CC*), and the *rule priority* (*RP*). These parameters are measures reflecting the *uncertainties* that we associate with each and every rule in the knowledge base.

We refer to these measures of confidence as *subjective knowledge* because it is up to us to assign their values and the values of their relative weights (see below) to each rule, and we do so based on our subjective judgement.

The parameters *RP* and *RC* are used to evaluate the overall weight of each rule with respect to the other rules in the knowledge base. If we let $W_{RP}$ and $W_{RC}$ be the weights associated with *RP* and *RC*, respectively, then the *overall weight* $W_{R_n}$ of rule $R_n$ is a measure of our overall confidence in that rule, and it is given by the expression:

$$W_{R_n} = \frac{W_{RP} \cdot RP + W_{RC} \cdot RC}{W_{RP} + W_{RC}} \qquad (7.1)$$

The conclusion confidence (*CC*) parameter is used in the inference process as a measure of the relationship between the premise and the conclusion of any given rule. We defer the discussion of its role in the inference process to Chapter 10.

It is important to note that the three confidence (uncertainty) measures need not be equally weighted. In fact, we may assign them different weights to reflect the fact that each one of them can have a different impact on the decision-making process.


## 7.2 Procedures For Knowledge Processing

In this section we show how to parse a rule and how to generate the data structure that includes the interpreted meaning of the fuzzy clauses of each rule.

In general, production rules in the knowledge base (see Chapter 5) can consist of three types of clauses.

1.  executable procedures

2.  regular sentences

3.  mathematical expressions.

It should be noted that executable procedures and mathematical expressions are executed *only* when the inference engine is invoked. In the preprocessing stage, the expert system shell does not evaluate these expressions but flags them so that the inference engine will know what type of clauses they are and whether or not they are *potentially* linked to other clauses.

We consider these three types of clauses in the following paragraphs.


### 7.2.1 Executable Procedures

Executable procedures are very useful, powerful features of any expert system. The general format of an executable procedure is:

{*procedure_name; parameters*}

and is used whenever we want to link the knowledge base with some executable code. For example, the rule:

*If object-1 is not recognized, Then {RECOGNIZE(object-1, CF)}*

states that if some object is not yet recognized, then the procedure *RECOGNIZE* is invoked to perform the recognition process of the object. The variable *CF* designates the *certainty factor* associated with the execution of the procedure. The results from the executable procedure are placed on the *blackboard*.

Incorporating the feature of executable procedures in the expert system implies that the expert system designer has a set of procedures linked to the expert system. Note, however, that in order to execute these procedures, the expert system must incorporate a compiler to parse the request and to link (or call) the proper procedure.

### 7.2.2 Regular Sentences

The general structure of a clause in regular sentences is:

*X is Y*

where $X$ is the subject and $Y$ is the object. When we process clauses of this type, we have to distinguish between clauses without fuzzy variables and clauses with fuzzy variables.

#### Clauses Without Fuzzy Variables

The object $Y$ in clauses without fuzzy variables can be a *word*, a *number*, or a *real interval*. To process such clauses, we associate the object $Y$ with two bounding intervals, referred to as the object's *dual interval*, $[lb_1, ub_1]$ and $[lb_2, ub_2]$, where $lb$ and $ub$ stand for lower bound and upper bound, respectively.

Since the object may be modified and/or negated, we must account for the modifier (MOD) and not (NOT) operators in the description of $Y$. Hence, we have to consider the following four types of clauses in a regular sentence:

- *X is Y*
- *X is MOD Y*
- *X is NOT Y*
- *X is NOT MOD Y*

Let us dwell briefly on these four cases in the following paragraphs.

1. *X is Y.* Since both the NOT operator and the modifier are off, we have the following.

    (a) If $Y$ is a word, then $lb_1 = ub_1 = 1$.

    (b) If $Y$ is a number $N$, then $lb_1 = ub_1 = N$.

(c) If $Y$ is a real interval $[N1, N2]$, then $lb_1 = N1$ and $ub_1 = N2$.

We see that in these three cases, both $lb_1$ and $ub_1$ receive a value whereas the lower and upper bounds of the second interval $[lb_2, ub_2]$ remain undefined.

2.  $X$ *is MOD* $Y$. Since the modifier modifies $Y$, we may apply it to any of the intervals generated in the previous case. To do so, let *COMPUTE_RANGE (MOD, NUM, LB, UB)* be a procedure that takes the modifier MOD and some number NUM as inputs and generates an interval $[LB, UB]$. Since the modifier is associated with an interval, let us designate the interval's lower bound and upper bound by $\downarrow$ and $\uparrow$, respectively.

The procedure *COMPUTE_RANGE* searches for the modifier in the modifier list, extracts the values associated with $\downarrow$ and $\uparrow$, and computes the lower and upper bounds of the interval $[LB, UB]$,

$$LB = NUM \cdot \downarrow$$

and

$$UB = NUM \cdot \uparrow$$

The values $LB$ and $UB$ generated by *COMPUTE_RANGE* are then assigned to the interval(s) obtained in Case 1 above, namely:

$$lb_1 = LB$$
$$ub_1 = UB$$

Note that, similarly to Case 1, here too the second interval $[lb_2, ub_2]$ remains undefined.

To illustrate this procedure, assume that MOD = *more_or_less* and NUM = 20. Also assume that *more_or_less* generates an interval that is $\pm10\%$ about NUM, namely, *more_or_less*$\downarrow$ = 0.9 and *more_or_less*$\uparrow$ = 1.1. Then, using the *COMPUTE_RANGE* procedure, we get:

$$LB = more\_or\_less\downarrow \cdot NUM$$
$$= 0.9 \cdot 20 = 18$$

and

$$UB = more\_or\_less\uparrow \cdot NUM$$
$$= 1.1 \cdot 20 = 22$$

Therefore, $lb_1 = LB = 18$ and $ub_1 = UB = 22$.

3.  $X$ *is NOT* $Y$. In this case we have to negate the interval(s) derived in Case 1. Let $\alpha$ and $\beta$ be the smallest number and the largest number, respectively, in the domain of $Y$. Then, the negation of $Y$ generates the following two distinct bounding intervals [84]:

$$[\alpha, \ lb_1 - \varepsilon]$$

and

$$[ub_1 + \varepsilon, \ \beta]$$

where $\varepsilon > 0$ is an arbitrarily small number used to guarantee that the intervals generated by negation will not intersect the original interval.

Hence, in the two bounding intervals generated by *NOT Y*, the lower and the upper bounds of the first interval are $\alpha$ and $lb_1-\varepsilon$, respectively, and the lower and upper bounds of the second interval are $ub_1+\varepsilon$ and $\beta$, respectively. That is:

$$lb_1 \leftarrow \alpha$$

$$ub_1 \leftarrow ub_1 - \varepsilon$$

$$lb_2 \leftarrow ub_1 + \varepsilon$$

$$ub_2 \leftarrow \beta$$

4. *X is NOT MOD Y.* This case can be evaluated in three steps. First, we create the proper interval(s) as described in Case 1. Then, following the procedure presented in Case 2, we compute the new interval with the modifier. Finally, we apply the NOT operation to this interval to generate the two distinct bounding intervals as shown in Case 3.

The following tables summarize the parsing process of regular sentences without fuzzy variables. The parsing of clauses in which the object $Y$ is a word, a number, or a real interval is presented in Tables 7.1 to 7.3, respectively.

In Tables 7.1 to 7.3, we use the following nomenclature:

| | | |
|---|---|---|
| $u$ | - | undefined field |
| $N$ | - | number |
| $N1$ | - | lower bound of the interval |
| $N2$ | - | upper bound of the interval |
| $\varepsilon$ | - | an arbitrarily small positive number |
| $\downarrow$ | - | lower bound of the modifier |
| $\uparrow$ | - | upper bound of the modifier |
| $\alpha$ | - | lower bound of the domain of $Y$ |
| $\beta$ | - | upper bound of the domain of $Y$ |

**Table 7.1** Parsing a clause where $Y$ is a word

| Clause Type | $Y$ is a word | | | |
|---|---|---|---|---|
| | $lb_1$ | $ub_1$ | $lb_2$ | $ub_2$ |
| $X$ is $Y$ | $1$ | $1$ | $u$ | $u$ |
| $X$ is MOD $Y$ | $1 \cdot \downarrow$ | $1 \cdot \uparrow$ | $u$ | $u$ |
| $X$ is NOT $Y$ | $0$ | $1 - \varepsilon$ | $1 + \varepsilon$ | $2$ |
| $X$ is NOT MOD $Y$ | $0$ | $(1 \cdot \downarrow) - \varepsilon$ | $(1 \cdot \uparrow) + \varepsilon$ | $2$ |

**Table 7.2** Parsing a clause where $Y$ is a number

| Clause Type | $Y$ is a number | | | |
|---|---|---|---|---|
| | $lb_1$ | $ub_1$ | $lb_2$ | $ub_2$ |
| $X$ is $Y$ | $N$ | $N$ | $u$ | $u$ |
| $X$ is MOD $Y$ | $N \cdot \downarrow$ | $N \cdot \uparrow$ | $u$ | $u$ |
| $X$ is NOT $Y$ | $\alpha$ | $N - \varepsilon$ | $N + \varepsilon$ | $\beta$ |
| $X$ is NOT MOD $Y$ | $\alpha$ | $(N \cdot \downarrow) - \varepsilon$ | $(N \cdot \uparrow) + \varepsilon$ | $\beta$ |

**Table 7.3** Parsing a clause where $Y$ is a real interval

| Clause Type | $Y$ is an interval | | | |
|---|---|---|---|---|
| | $lb_1$ | $ub_1$ | $lb_2$ | $ub_2$ |
| $X$ is $Y$ | $N1$ | $N1$ | $u$ | $u$ |
| $X$ is MOD $Y$ | $N1 \cdot \downarrow$ | $N2 \cdot \uparrow$ | $u$ | $u$ |
| $X$ is NOT $Y$ | $\alpha$ | $N1 - \varepsilon$ | $N2 + \varepsilon$ | $\beta$ |
| $X$ is NOT MOD $Y$ | $\alpha$ | $(N1 \cdot \downarrow) - \varepsilon$ | $(N2 \cdot \uparrow) + \varepsilon$ | $\beta$ |

### Clauses With Fuzzy Variables

Unlike clauses without fuzzy variables, the object $Y$ in clauses with fuzzy variables can be only a *word*, that is, it is a fuzzy variable associated with a membership function.

However, since the object may be modified and/or negated, then similarly to clauses without fuzzy variables, here too we have to consider the following four types of clauses:

- *X is Y*
- *X is MOD Y*
- *X is NOT Y*
- *X is NOT MOD Y*

To process these clauses, we must do three things.

1. Identify and associate the proper membership function with the fuzzy variable. That is, associate the fuzzy variable *Y* with the proper membership function (if one exists for that particular variable).

2. Identify whether or not the clause contains a modifier.

3. Flag the record containing the clause if the negation is present.

The intervals associated with the clauses with fuzzy variables remain undefined because they have no role in the matching process. Since every object is parsed according to Tables 7.1 - 7.3, a data structure is created in which the object of the clause is associated with some intervals. However, since the object of the clause is a fuzzy variable, the data structure created is not used in evaluting this type of clause.

## 7.2.3 Mathematical Functions

Expert systems are designed primarily to capture and process linguistic knowledge in an attempt to model the cognitive processes of the human mind. These processes can be modeled more closely by fuzzy expert systems because these systems can handle uncertain or imprecise linguistic knowledge.

However, in addition to linguistic knowledge, real world problems often include knowledge that can be expressed in some mathematical form. For example, we may wish to know how far is it to the grocery store if we have to walk "*about* 1 mile due north and *almost* ¾ mile due east." To deal with this kind of knowledge, as well as with the uncertainty in numeric data, we have to expand the domain of the fuzzy expert system.

To handle knowledge expressed in mathematical form within the fuzzy expert system calls for the use of *interval arithmetic*. Interval arithmetic was developed as a way to bound errors inherent in calculations performed in a digital computer [30] and resulting from a combination of round-off, truncation, and limited machine precision [66].

The use of intervals is the simplest method for propagating uncertainty through arithmetic calculations. If we are unsure about the exact value of some variable, we can still specify the variable by using an interval which represents the range of values that the variable may take.

Interval arithmetic is an extension of real arithmetic in which the standard operators (+, −, ·, /) are applied to intervals of real numbers rather than to the real numbers themselves. The intervals are carried out through all the calculations and result in an interval that exactly bounds the answer [67].

An *interval X* is a closed, bounded set of real numbers,

$$\{x \mid \underline{X} \leq x \leq \overline{X}, \ x \in X\}$$

designated as $X = [\underline{X}, \overline{X}]$, where $\underline{X}$ and $\overline{X}$ are the interval's endpoints (the lower and upper bounds of $X$, respectively). The *width* of $X$, $w(X)$, is given by:

$$w(X) = \overline{X} - \underline{X} + \varepsilon \tag{7.2}$$

where the constant $\varepsilon$ is an arbitrarily small, positive number that we add to prevent $w(X)$ from being $0$ in the special case when $X$ is a *singleton*. In this special case, since $\overline{X} = \underline{X}$, $w(X)$ would be $0$ unless $\varepsilon$ is added to yield $w(X) = \varepsilon$.

The *intersection* of two intervals, $X = [\underline{X}, \overline{X}]$ and $Y = [\underline{Y}, \overline{Y}]$, is the interval given by:

$$[X \cap Y] = \begin{cases} \varnothing & \text{If } \underline{X} > \overline{Y} \text{ or } \underline{Y} > \overline{X} \\ [max(\underline{X}, \underline{Y}), \ min(\overline{X}, \overline{Y})] & \text{Otherwise} \end{cases} \tag{7.3}$$

where $\varnothing$ designates an *empty* intersection.

With this brief introduction, let us turn now to mathematical functions. The general format of a *mathematical function* is:

$$[ \ expression \ ]$$

where we distinguish between two types of expressions:

1.    arithmetic expressions

2.    logical expressions

In the following paragraphs we describe the procedures for evaluating these two types of mathematical expressions.


*Evaluating Arithmetic Expressions*

Assignment statements for arithmetic expressions are used *only* in the conclusion parts of the rules and have the following form:

$$[X := math\_expression]$$

For example, the assignment statement $[X := sqr(Y)]$ computes the square of the variable $Y$ and assigns it to the variable $X$.

To extend the application of the arithmetic operations $(+, -, \cdot, /)$ to intervals of real numbers, consider the two intervals $X = [\underline{X}, \overline{X}]$ and $Y = [\underline{Y}, \overline{Y}]$. Then, the rules of interval arithmetic are as follows.

- *Addition*:

$$[X + Y] = [min(A), max(A)]$$

where the set $A$ is given by

$$A = (\underline{X} + \underline{Y}, \underline{X} + \overline{Y}, \overline{X} + \underline{Y}, \overline{X} + \overline{Y})$$

- *Subtraction*:

$$[X - Y] = [min(B), max(B)]$$

where the set $B$ is given by

$$B = (\underline{X} - \underline{Y}, \underline{X} - \overline{Y}, \overline{X} - \underline{Y}, \overline{X} - \overline{Y})$$

- *Multiplication*:

$$[X \cdot Y] = [min(C), max(C)]$$

where the set $C$ is given by

$$C = (\underline{X} \cdot \underline{Y}, \underline{X} \cdot \overline{Y}, \overline{X} \cdot \underline{Y}, \overline{X} \cdot \overline{Y})$$

- *Division*:

$$[X / Y] = [min(D), max(D)]$$

where the set $D$ is given by

$$D = (\underline{X}/\underline{Y}, \underline{X}/\overline{Y}, \overline{X}/\underline{Y}, \overline{X}/\overline{Y})$$

Notice that the operation $[X / Y]$ is undefined if $\underline{Y} = 0$, $\overline{Y} = 0$, or if both $\underline{Y}$ and $\overline{Y}$ are $0$.

Finally, if $F$ is some function on the interval $X = [\underline{X}, \overline{X}]$, then the resulting interval $[F(X)]$ is given by:

$$[F(X)] = [min(F(\underline{X}), F(\overline{X})), max(F(\underline{X}), F(\overline{X}))]$$

**Example 7.1:** To illustrate interval arithmetic operations, consider the interval $X = [10, 15]$ and the singleton $Y = 20$ (or, alternatively, the interval $Y = [20, 20]$). Then, following the above derivations, we have:

$$[X + Y] = [min(30, 30, 35, 35), max(30, 30, 35, 35)]$$
$$= [30, 35]$$

$$[X - Y] = [min(-10, -10, -5, -5), max(-10, -10, -5, -5)]$$
$$= [-10, -5]$$

$$[X \cdot Y] = [min(200, 200, 300, 300), max(200, 200, 300, 300)]$$
$$= [200, 300]$$

$$[X / Y] = [min(0.5, 0.5, 0.75, 0.75), max(0.5, 0.5, 0.75, 0.75)]$$
$$= [0.5, 0.75]$$

### Evaluating Logical Expressions

The relational operators $(=, \neq, <, \leq, >, \geq)$ define logical relations between pairs of intervals. Logical relations between fuzzy sets have already been implemented in the expert system FLOPS [89], however, they cannot be applied directly in our case. Instead, we present a method for evaluating logical relations between intervals as an extension of the fuzzy inferencing algorithm in [48] and [86].

In Chapter 10, we describe the algorithm for evaluating logical expressions in the context of the inference process. This algorithm is based on the mathematical foundation prepared in this section.

*Logical expressions* are used *only* in the premise part of the rules and have the following form:

$$[X <op> Y]$$

where $X$ and $Y$ are mathematical expressions and $<op>$ is some logical relation between them. For simplicity, we will assume in the following discussion that both $X$ and $Y$ are variables represented by intervals.

To set the discussion going, consider the following problem:

*Given two intervals, $X = [\underline{X}, \overline{X}]$ and $Y = [\underline{Y}, \overline{Y}]$, what is the probability that, for any two real numbers $x \in X$ and $y \in Y$, $x <op> y$ is true, where $<op>$ is a logical operator in the set $(=, \neq, <, \leq, >, \geq)$?*

This is an important and practical question when we deal with intervals in expert systems. To illustrate it, assume two clauses

$$X = John \ is \ 20 \ to \ 30 \ years \ old$$
$$Y = Jim \ is \ 27 \ to \ 33 \ years \ old$$

and a rule that states:

*If [X > Y] Then ...*

The expert system must determine who is older, John or Jim, even though we are unsure about their exact ages and have, therefore, specified them as intervals. Indeed, as was mentioned earlier, the use of intervals is the simplest method for propagating uncertainty through arithmetic calculations.

So the question pertaining to the relationships among clauses specified by intervals is a pertinent one. We can rephrase the question using our example, in which we want to know who is older, John or Jim, by asking what is the probability that John is older than Jim?

Let us begin by considering the case of $x = y$. If $X \cap Y = \emptyset$, then the probability that $x = y$ is 0. On the other hand, if $X \cap Y \neq \emptyset$, then denoting the portion of $X$ in $X \cap Y$ as $X_I$ and the portion of $Y$ in $X \cap Y$ as $Y_I$, the probability that $x = \xi$, where $\xi \in X_I$, is given by:

$$P(x = \xi) = \frac{\varepsilon}{w(X_I)}, \quad \xi \in X_I \tag{7.4a}$$

where $\varepsilon > 0$ is some arbitrarily small number and $w(X_I)$ is the *width* of $X_I$ (see Equation (7.2)). Similarly, the probability that $y = \xi$, where $\xi \in Y_I$, is given by:

$$P(y = \xi) = \frac{\varepsilon}{w(Y_I)}, \quad \xi \in Y_I \tag{7.4b}$$

where $w(Y_I)$ is the *width* of $Y_I$. Note that in this case, $X_I = Y_I$ and, therefore, the two probabilities, $P(x=\xi)$ and $P(y=\xi)$, are equal. Also note that we implicitly assume that $w(X_I) = w(Y_I) \neq 0$.

Consider now the probabilities of $x$ and $y$ falling within the intersections $X_I$ and $Y_I$, respectivly. Let $w(X)$ and $w(Y)$ designate the widths of the intervals $X$ and $Y$, respectively, then the probability that any $x$ falls within the intersection $X_I$ is given by:

$$P(x \in X_I) = \frac{w(X_I)}{w(X)} \tag{7.5a}$$

whereas the probability that any $y$ falls within the intersection $Y_I$ is given by:

$$P(y \in Y_I) = \frac{w(Y_I)}{w(Y)} \tag{7.5b}$$

Furthermore, we have to take this into consideration the fact that $\xi$ can be any number within any of the two intersections. Hence, if we designate by $\eta$ the number of different $\xi$ inside $X_I$ (we consider only $X_I$ since $X_I = Y_I$), then:

$$\eta = \frac{w(X_I)}{\varepsilon} \tag{7.6}$$

Combining Equations (7.4) - (7.6), we conclude that the probability of $x = y$ and $\xi \in X_I$ is given by:

$$P(x = y) = P(x = \xi)_{|\xi \in X_I} \cdot P(y = \xi)_{|\xi \in Y_I} \cdot P(x \in X_I) \cdot P(y \in Y_I) \cdot \eta$$

$$= \frac{\varepsilon \cdot w(X_I)}{w(X) \cdot w(Y)} \tag{7.7}$$

**Example 7.2:** Let $X = [5, 8]$, $Y = [6, 10]$, and $\varepsilon = 10^{-10}$. From Equation (7.2), we get $w(X) = 3$ and $w(Y) = 4$. To compute $w(X_I)$, we use Equation (7.3) to find $[X \cap Y] = [6, 8]$ and Equation (7.2) to get $w(X_I) = 2$. Then, using Equation (7.7), we obtain $P(x = y) = 1.6667 \times 10^{-11} \approx 0$ for *any* real numbers $x$ and $y$ within the intervals $X$ and $Y$.

We can easily verify that Equation (7.7) also holds when the intervals $X$ and $Y$ are singletons. In this case, $\underline{X} = \overline{X}$, and $\underline{Y} = \overline{Y}$ and, therefore, $w(X) = w(Y) = \varepsilon$. Hence, if $X$ and $Y$ intersect, then the probability of $x = y$ is given by:

$$P(x = y) = \frac{\varepsilon^2}{w(X) \cdot w(Y)} = \frac{\varepsilon^2}{\varepsilon^2} = 1 \tag{7.8}$$

as expected.

Finally, the complement of $P(x = y)$ is given by:

$$P(x \neq y) = 1 - P(x = y)$$

$$= 1 - \frac{\varepsilon \cdot w(X_I)}{w(X) \cdot w(Y)} \tag{7.9}$$

Let us now consider the probability that $x < y$. There are six different cases for which we must compute $P(x < y)$, the probability that $x < y$. As you will see shortly in the listing of these cases, whenever we have intersecting intervals, we compute $P(x < y)$ using constituent probabilities designated as $P(x < y)_I$, $P(x < y)_P$, and $P(x < y)_F$. These probability components pertain respectively to the following instances: (i) $x$ and $y$ are in $X_I = X \cap Y$ and $x < y$ is within the intersection; (ii) $x$ precedes the intersecting interval; and (iii) $x$ is in the intersecting interval and $y$ follows.

Illustrated below are the six possible cases for calculating $P(x < y)$:

**Case 1.** The intervals $X$ and $Y$ do not intersect and the entire interval of $X$ precedes the entire interval of $Y$. Hence,

$$P(x < y) = 1$$

_____X_____

                                    _____Y_____

**Case 2.** The intervals $X$ and $Y$ intersect, with $X$ preceding $Y$. $P(x < y)$ is the probability that $x$ precedes $X \cap Y$, or $x < y$ is within $X \cap Y$, or $x$ is in $X \cap Y$ and $y$ follows. Hence,

$$P(x < y) = P(x < y)_I + P(x < y)_P + P(x < y)_F$$

$$\underline{\hspace{6cm}X\hspace{6cm}}$$

$$\underline{\hspace{6cm}Y\hspace{6cm}}$$

**Case 3.** In this case, $P(x < y)$ is the probability that $x$ precedes $X \cap Y$, or $x < y$ is within $X \cap Y$. That is,

$$P(x < y) = P(x < y)_I + P(x < y)_P$$

$$\underline{\hspace{7cm}X\hspace{7cm}}$$

$$\underline{\hspace{3cm}Y\hspace{3cm}}$$

**Case 4.** In this case, $P(x < y)$ is the probability that $x < y$ within $X \cap Y$, or $x$ is in $X \cap Y$ and $y$ follows. Hence,

$$P(x < y) = P(x < y)_I + P(x < y)_F$$

$$\underline{\hspace{2cm}X\hspace{2cm}}$$

$$\underline{\hspace{6cm}Y\hspace{6cm}}$$

**Case 5.** Here, since $x < y$ is within $X \cap Y$, then:

$$P(x < y) = P(x < y)_I$$

$$\underline{\hspace{5cm}X\hspace{5cm}}$$

$$\underline{\hspace{5cm}Y\hspace{5cm}}$$

**Case 6.** In this case, since the entire interval of $X$ follows the entire interval of $Y$, we have:

$$P(x < y) = 0$$

$$\underline{\hspace{5cm}X\hspace{5cm}}$$

$$\underline{\hspace{5cm}Y\hspace{5cm}}$$

Cases 2, 3, 4, and 5 involve intersecting intervals for which $P(x < y)$ is computed using the constituent probabilities $P(x < y)_I$, $P(x < y)_P$, and $P(x < y)_F$. Notice that the probability that $x < y$ is given by: $\dfrac{w(X_1)}{w(X)}$, the probability that some $x \in X \cap Y$; by

$\dfrac{w(Y_1)}{w(Y)} = \dfrac{w(X_1)}{w(X)}$, the probability that some $y$ is in $X \cap Y$; and by the probability that $x < y$ in $X \cap Y$. Because we have no information on the distribution of values of $x$ and $y$ within their respective intervals, we assume that they are evenly distributed. Therefore, there is an almost even chance that $x < y$ within the interval of intersection, namely:

$$P(x < y) \approx 0.5$$

Hence, the probability that $x, y \in X \cap Y$ and $x < y \in X \cap Y$ is given by:

$$P(x < y)_1 = \frac{1}{2} \cdot \frac{w(X_1)}{w(X)} \cdot \frac{w(X_1)}{w(Y)}$$

$$= \frac{1}{2} \cdot \frac{w(X_1)^2}{w(X) \cdot w(Y)} \qquad (7.10)$$

Equation (7.10) requires the calculation of $w(X_I)$, $X_I = X \cap Y$. To do so, we have to account for four possible intersections:

1.    $w(X_1) = \overline{X} - \underline{Y}$

2.    $w(X_1) = \overline{Y} - \underline{Y}$

3.    $w(X_1) = \overline{X} - \underline{X}$

4.    $w(X_1) = \overline{Y} - \underline{X}$

Note that for *Case 1*, in which the entire interval $X$ is smaller than the entire interval $Y$, the first difference, $\overline{X} - \underline{Y}$, is always be negative, indicating that there is no intersection and, therefore, $w(X_I) = 0$. Similarly, for *Case 6*, in which the entire interval $Y$ is smaller than the entire interval $X$, the fourth difference, $\overline{Y} - \underline{X}$, is always be negative, again indicating that there is no intersection so that $w(X_I) = 0$. Thus, a negative diffrence implies no interval of intersection; otherwise, the minimum of the four differences is the actual interval of intersection.

Hence, to calculate $w(X_I)$ for *Cases 2, 3, 4,* and *5* (which involve intersecting intervals), we have to take the *minimum* of the four differences and then the *maximum* between this minimum and 0. In other words,

$$w(X_1) = max(min(\overline{X} - \underline{Y}, \overline{Y} - \underline{Y}, \overline{X} - \underline{X}, \overline{Y} - \underline{X}), \, 0) \qquad (7.11)$$

Then, substituting Equation (7.11) into Equation (7.10), we get:

$$P(x < y)_1 = \frac{(max(min(\overline{X} - \underline{Y}, \overline{Y} - \underline{Y}, \overline{X} - \underline{X}, \overline{Y} - \underline{X}), \, 0))^2}{2 \cdot w(X) \cdot w(Y)} \qquad (7.12)$$

Notice that Equations (7.10) and (7.12) hold even if either $X$ or $Y$ have single point values. To see this, let $X = Y$ and use Equation (7.12) to establish that $P(x < y)_I = 0$.

Consider now the evaluation of $P(x < y)_P$, the probability that $x$ precedes $X \cap Y$ while $y$ follows $x$:

(a) In *Case 1*, $w(X_I) = 0$ since $X$ completely precedes $Y$ and, therefore, $P(x < y)_P = \dfrac{w(X)}{w(X)} = 1$. Conversely, $Y$ completely follows $X$ so that the probability that $y$ follows $x$ is $\dfrac{w(Y)}{w(Y)} = 1$.

(b) For *Cases 2 and 3*, $X$ precedes $X_I$ by $\underline{Y} - \underline{X}$ and therefore, $P(x < y)_P = \dfrac{\underline{Y} - \underline{X}}{w(X)}$.

Again, since $x$ precedes $X_I$, we see that the probability that $y$ follows $x$ is 1.

(c) For *Cases 4, 5 and 6*, $x$ never precedes $X_I$ and, since the probability that $y$ follows $x$ is irrelevant, we get $P(x < y)_P = 0$.

Combining these results, we obtain:

$$P(x < y)_P = \frac{min(w(X), \; max(\underline{Y} - \underline{X}, \; 0))}{w(X)} \cdot \frac{w(Y)}{w(Y)} \qquad (7.13)$$

Finally, to evaluate $P(x < y)_F$, the probability that $x$ is in $X_I$ and $y$ follows, we note that:

(a) In *Cases 1 and 6*, $w(X_I) = 0$ so that $P(x < y)_F = 0$.

(b) In *Cases 3 and 5*, no part of $Y$ follows $X_I$ so, again, $P(x < y)_F = 0$.

(c) For *Cases 2 and 4*, the amount of $Y$ following $X_I$ is $\overline{Y} - \overline{X}$ and, therefore, $P(x < y)_F = \dfrac{\overline{Y} - \overline{X}}{w(Y)}$.

Hence, since we know that the probability that $x$ is in $X_I$ is $\dfrac{w(X_I)}{w(X)}$, and the probability that $y$ follows $X_I$ for all six cases is $\dfrac{max(\overline{Y} - \overline{X}, \; 0)}{w(Y)}$, then:

$$P(x < y)_F = \frac{w(X_I)}{w(X)} \cdot \frac{max(\overline{Y} - \overline{X}, 0)}{w(Y)} \qquad (7.14)$$

We can now summarize our results in a combined form:

$$P(x < y) = P(x < y)_I + P(x < y)_P + P(x < y)_F \qquad (7.15)$$

where the constituent probabilities are given in Equations (7.12), (7.13), and (7.14), respectively. The following two examples illustrate our results.

**Example 7.3:** Consider the intervals $X = [0, 8]$ and $Y = [5, 10]$ that are illustrated in the following diagram:

$X \quad 0$ ———————————————————— $8$

$Y$ ———————————— $5$ ———————————— $10$

Using Equations (7.12), (7.13), and (7.14), we get:

$$P(x < y)_I = \frac{(max(min(3, 5, 8, 10), 0))^2}{2 \cdot 8 \cdot 5} = \frac{9}{80}$$

$$P(x < y)_P = \frac{min(8, \ max(5 - 0, \ 0))}{8} = \frac{5}{8}$$

$$P(x < y)_F = \frac{3}{8} \cdot \frac{max(10 - 8, \ 0)}{5} = \frac{6}{40}$$

Substituting these results into Equation (7.15), we obtain:

$$P(x < y) = \frac{9}{80} + \frac{5}{8} + \frac{6}{40} = 0.89$$

indicating that we are 89% confident that $x < y$.

**Example 7.4:** This example illustrates what happens when the values of $X$ and $Y$ in Example 7.3 are inter-changed. Consider, therefore, the intervals $X = [5, 10]$ and $Y = [0, 8]$ that are depicted in the diagram below. In this case, Equations (7.12), (7.13), and (7.14) yield:

$X$ ———————————— $5$ ———————————— $10$

$Y \quad 0$ ———————————————————— $8$

$$P(x < y)_I = \frac{(max(min(10, 8, 5, 3), 0))^2}{2 \cdot 8 \cdot 5} = \frac{9}{80}$$

$$P(x < y)_P = \frac{min(5, \ max(0 - 5, \ 0))}{5} = \frac{0}{5} = 0$$

$$P(x < y)_F = \frac{3}{5} \cdot \frac{max(8 - 10, \ 0)}{8} = \frac{0}{40} = 0$$

Substituting these results into Equation (7.15), we get:

$$P(x < y) = \frac{9}{80} = 0.11$$

As we can see, we are now only 11% confident that $x < y$.

To complete our discussion, we have to evaluate $P(x \leq y)$, $P(x > y)$, and $P(x \geq y)$. To derive an equation for $P(x \leq y)$, note that $P(x \leq y)$ equals $P(x < y)$ or the probability that $x = y$ within the interval of intersection $X \cap Y$. Hence:

$$P(x \leq y) = P(x < y) + P(x = y) \tag{7.16}$$

A similar argument can be made for the logical relations $x > y$ and $x \geq y$. Computing $P(x > y)$ is straightforward and is obtained by:

$$P(x > y) = 1 - P(x \leq y) \tag{7.17}$$

whereas the derivation of $P(x \geq y)$ follows from Equation (7.15):

$$P(x \geq y) = 1 - P(x < y) \tag{7.18}$$

As was mentioned in Section 7.2.2, processing clauses in regular sentences calls for double intervals. To deal with this case, observe that the probability of $x <op> y$ can be expressed as the sum of the probabilities of every combination of each sub-interval of $X$ and $Y$, namely:

1. $X_1$ and $Y_1$

2. $X_1$ and $Y_2$

3. $X_2$ and $Y_1$

4. $X_2$ and $Y_2$

In general, if $N$ is the number of intervals in $X$ and $M$ is the number of intervals in $Y$, then $P(x <op> y)$ for multiple intervals can be expressed as:

$$P(x < op > y) = \sum_{i=1}^{N} \sum_{j=1}^{M} P(X_i < op > Y_j) \tag{7.19}$$

Consequently, if we let $X_{1_{ij}}$ represent the intersection of $X_i$ and $Y_j$ [98], then following Equation (7.7), we get:

$$P(x = y) = \sum_{i=1}^{N} \sum_{j=1}^{M} C_0 \cdot \frac{\varepsilon \cdot w(X_{1_{ij}})}{w(X) \cdot w(Y)} \tag{7.20}$$

where

$$C_o = \begin{cases} 1 & \text{if } w(X_{1_{ij}}) > 0 \\ 0 & \text{if } w(X_{1_{ij}}) = 0 \end{cases}$$

and, following Equation (7.13),

$$w(X_{1_{ij}}) = max(min(\overline{X}_i - \underline{Y}_j, \overline{Y}_j - \underline{Y}_j, \overline{X}_i - \underline{X}_i, \overline{Y}_j - \underline{X}_i), 0) \qquad (7.21)$$

From Equation (7.9) we have:

$$P(x \neq y) = 1 - P(x = y) \qquad (7.22)$$

and Equations (7.10), (7.11), and (7.12) yield:

$$P(x < y) = \sum_{i=1}^{N} \sum_{j=1}^{M} C_i \cdot \frac{w(X_{1_{ij}})^2}{w(X) \cdot w(Y)} + \frac{min(w(X_i), \ max(\underline{Y}_j - \underline{X}_i, \ 0))}{w(X)} \cdot \frac{w(Y_j)}{w(Y)}$$

$$+ \frac{w(X_{1_{ij}})}{w(X)} \cdot \frac{max(\overline{Y}_j - \overline{X}_i, \ 0)}{w(Y)} \qquad (7.23)$$

where

$$C_i = \begin{cases} 0 & \text{if } w(X) = \varepsilon \ \text{ or } \ w(Y) = \varepsilon \\ \dfrac{1}{2} & \text{if } w(X) > \varepsilon \ \text{ and } w(Y) > \varepsilon \end{cases}$$

Note that in Equation (7.23), the first term corresponds to $P(x < y)_I$, the second term corresponds to $P(x < y)_P$, and the third term corresponds to $P(x < y)_F$. The following example illustrates these results.

**Example 7.5:** Let $X = [2, 10] [12, 15]$ and $Y = [5, 11] [13, 17]$, and refer to the diagram below.

| X | 2 | | | 10 | 12 | | 15 | |
|---|---|---|---|---|---|---|---|---|

| Y | | 5 | | | 11 | 13 | | 17 |
|---|---|---|---|---|---|---|---|---|

Designating by $X_1$ and $X_2$ the lower and upper sub-intervals of $X$, respectively, and by $Y_1$ and $Y_2$ the lower and upper sub-intervals of $Y$, respectively, we have: $X_1 = [2, 10]$, $w(X_1) = 8$; $X_2 = [12, 15]$, $w(X_2) = 3$; $Y_1 = [5, 11]$, $w(Y_1) = 6$; $Y_2 = [13, 17]$, $w(Y_2) = 4$. Also, $w(X) = w(X_1) + w(X_2) = 11$ and $w(Y) = w(Y_1) + w(Y_2) = 10$.

To obtain a confidence factor for $x < y$, we apply Equations (7.21) and (7.23):

- *For $X_1$ and $Y_1$:*

$$P(x<y)_I = \frac{(max(min(10-5,\ 11-5,\ 10-2,\ 11-2),\ 0))^2}{2\cdot 11\cdot 10} = \frac{25}{220}$$

$$P(x<y)_P = \frac{6}{10}\cdot\frac{min(8,\ max(5-2,\ 0))}{11} = \frac{18}{110}$$

$$P(x<y)_F = \frac{5}{11}\cdot\frac{max(11-10,\ 0)}{10} = \frac{5}{110}$$

Hence, $P_{1,1}(x<y) = 71/220$.

- *For $X_1$ and $Y_2$:*

$$P(x<y)_I = \frac{(max(min(10-13,\ 17-13,\ 10-2,\ 17-2),\ 0))^2}{2\cdot 11\cdot 10} = 0$$

$$P(x<y)_P = \frac{4}{10}\cdot\frac{min(8,\ max(13-2,\ 0))}{11} = \frac{32}{110}$$

$$P(x<y)_F = \frac{0}{11}\cdot\frac{max(17-10,\ 0)}{10} = 0$$

Hence, $P_{1,2}(x<y) = 64/220$.

- *For $X_2$ and $Y_1$:.*

$$P(x<y)_I = \frac{(max(min(15-5,\ 11-5,\ 15-12,\ 11-12),\ 0))^2}{2\cdot 11\cdot 10} = 0$$

$$P(x<y)_P = \frac{6}{10}\cdot\frac{min(3,\ max(5-12,\ 0))}{11} = 0$$

$$P(x<y)_F = \frac{0}{11}\cdot\frac{max(11-15,\ 0)}{10} = 0$$

Hence, $P_{2,1}(x<y) = 0$

- *For $X_2$ and $Y_2$:*

$$P(x<y)_I = \frac{(max(min(15-13,\ 17-13,\ 15-12,\ 17-12),\ 0))^2}{2\cdot 11\cdot 10} = \frac{4}{220}$$

$$P(x<y)_P = \frac{4}{10}\cdot\frac{min(3,\ max(13-12,\ 0))}{11} = \frac{4}{110}$$

$$P(x < y)_F = \frac{2}{11} \cdot \frac{max(17 - 15,\, 0)}{10} = \frac{4}{110}$$

Hence, $P_{2,2}(x < y) = 20/220$.

Combining these partial results, we obtain the *total confidence factor* for $x < y$:

$$P(x < y) = P_{1,1}(x < y) + P_{1,2}(x < y) + P_{2,1}(x < y) + P_{2,2}(x < y)$$

$$= 0.70$$

It follows then that we are 70% confident that $x < y$.

## 7.3 Relations Between Production Rules

The *relational list* (R-list), introduced in Chapter 5, is a knowledge representation structure particularly adept for representing knowledge in fuzzy expert systems. The R-list is a 6-tuple listing of the relations among the rules in the knowledge base:

$$R\text{-}list = (R_i,\, C_j,\, R_k,\, C_l,\, MF,\, MG) \tag{7.24}$$

where $R_i$ and $C_j$ are the *i*th rule and the *j*th clause in the *conclusion* of $R_i$, respectively; $R_k$ and $C_l$ are the *k*th rule and the *l*th clause in *premise* of $R_k$, respectively; and $MF$ and $MG$ are two parameters respectively indicating the *degree of similarity* between the two clauses and the *degree of membership* of one clause with respect to the other.

Each row in the R-list is interpreted as follows.

> *Clause $C_j$ in the conclusion of rule $R_i$ is similar to the clause $C_l$ in the premise of rule $R_k$ with degree of similarity MF and degree of membership MG.*

The degree of membership is defined as:

$$MG = \begin{cases} \chi_F(x) & \text{if } x \in F \\ -1 & \text{if there is a potential link between the two clauses} \\ -2 & \text{otherwise} \end{cases} \tag{7.25}$$

where $\chi_F(x)$ is the grade of membership of $x$ in $F$. The degree of similarity is defined as:

$$MF = \begin{cases} M & \text{if the matching can be evaluated during preprocessing} \\ -1 & \text{if there is a potential link between the two clauses} \end{cases} \tag{7.26}$$

where $M$ is the *matching factor*, $M \in [0,1]$, that indicates how well the two clauses match. Thus, $M = 1$ for a perfect match, whereas $M = 0$ indicates that the two clauses do not match at all. Any other value of $M$ indicates the degree to which the two clauses match.

We devote the remainder of this chapter to the process of matching clauses. Note that most current expert systems do not assign *certainty factors* (CF) dynamically but, instead, prompt the user to assign them. For example, if the knowledge base contains the rule:

*If John is between 20 and 30, Then John is young*

then the expert system would probably prompt the user with the question:

*What is the certainty factor that John is between 20 and 30?*

The user, in turn, provides a number between 0 and 1, say 0.8, and if this number is greater than a certain threshold, the rule fires with the conclusion:

*John is young with CF = 0.8*

Some expert systems assign the certainty factor to the conclusion but require a complete match between clauses. This means that if the clauses match, the certainty factor of the conclusion is assigned *a priori*, and if the clauses do not match, the rule does not fire. For example, if the user provides data that match the premise of the rule:

*If John is between 20 and 30, Then John is young with CF = 0.9*

then the truth of the conclusion will be 0.9; otherwise, it will be zero.

In contrast, we approach the *matching process* differently by suggesting a novel procedure for matching clauses and for using the matching factor $M$, which indicates the degree to which clauses match, to assign certainty factors to the conclusion dynamically.

In the following sections we show how to match different types of clauses, and how to assign the results to the R-list. In these sections, $R_C$, $M_C$, and $E_C$ denote regular, mathematical, and executable clauses, respectively. Since a regular clause may or may not be associated with a membership function (see Section 7.2.2), we denote by $R_c^M$ a regular clause associated with a membership function, and by $R_c^{\overline{M}}$ a regular clause that is not associated with a membership function.

## 7.3.1 Matching Mathematical Clauses With Mathematical Clauses

In the construction of the R-list, we compare a conclusion clause against a premise clause. This implies that of the two $M_C$ clauses, one clause must be an assignment statement,

$$[X := expression]$$

whereas the other clause must be a logical expression,

$$[\zeta < op > \psi]$$

However, since the logical expression contains at least one variable whose value cannot be determined during preprocessing, the parameters $MF$ and $MG$ are determined as follows:

$$MF = \begin{cases} 0 & \text{if } X \notin \zeta, \psi \\ -1 & \text{if } X \in \zeta, \psi \end{cases} \tag{7.27}$$

and

$$MG = -2 \tag{7.28}$$

Note that the parameter $MG$ is set to $-2$ because the clauses are not associated with membership functions.

## 7.3.2 Matching Regular Clauses With Regular Clauses

The matching process between two $R_c^{\overline{M}}$ clauses (namely, regular clauses that are not associated with membership functions) is based on the parsing procedure described in Section 7.2.2, and is divided into two parts. First, we try to match the objects in the clauses or their synonyms. If we are successful, then in the second part of the matching process, we match the quantitative values associated with the objects of each clause.

Let the two regular clauses be:

$$c_1: X \text{ is } Y$$

and

$$c_2: X^* \text{ is } Y^*$$

where the subject $Y$, or $Y^*$, can be a *word*, a *number*, an *interval*, or a *dual interval*. Hence, we can classify the matching process into three classes: (i) both subjects are words, (ii) only one subject is a word, and (iii) none of the subjects are words.

In the following paragraphs we address the matching process according to this classification. Note that $MF$ is the only parameter relevant here, whereas the parameter $MG$ is set to $-2$ in all three cases.

1.  *Both subjects are words.* In this case,

$$M = 1 \text{ if } X = X^* \text{ and } Y = Y^* \tag{7.29}$$

and, therefore, $MF = 1$.
However, if $c_2: X^* \text{ is NOT } Y^*$, then:

$$M = \begin{cases} 1 & \text{if } X = X^* \text{ and } Y \neq Y^* \\ 0 & \text{otherwise} \end{cases} \tag{7.30}$$

and, therefore, *MF* is also either *1* or *0*.

**Example 7.6:** Consider the clauses:

*Pressure is high*

*Pressure is high*

where *high* is *not* a fuzzy variable. Hence, $MG = -2$ and $MF = 1$ since the two clauses match perfectly.

2. *One subject is a word and the other is not.* In this case there cannot be a match and, therefore, $MF = 0$ and $MG = -2$, and the two clauses will not be linked in the R-list. For example, the following two clauses fall into this category:

*Pressure is high*

*Pressure is 60*

3. *None of the subjects are words.* In this case, Equation (7.26) reduces to $MF = M$. Since we have to match two clauses, and since each clause may contain two distinct intervals, we have to assume that there may be four intervals to consider. Therefore, let us designate the two intervals associated with the clause in the premise of the rule by *A* and *B*, and the two intervals associated with the clause in the conclusion by *C* and *D*.

Then, the *matching factor M* is computed using the following expression:

$$M = \frac{I(A,C) + I(A,D) + I(B,C) + I(B,D)}{w(C) + w(D)} \qquad (7.31)$$

In Equation (7.31), *w* designates the width of the interval (see Equation (7.2)), $w(m) = \overline{m} - \underline{m} + \varepsilon$, where $\overline{m}$ and $\underline{m}$ are the interval's endpoints (its upper and lower bounds, respectively), and $\varepsilon > 0$ is an arbitrarily small number.

The procedure $I(\cdot, \cdot)$ computes the intersection width of any two intervals [85], that is:

$$I(X,Y) = max(0, \ min(w(X), \ w(Y), \ \overline{Y} - \underline{X} + \varepsilon, \ \overline{X} - \underline{Y} + \varepsilon)) \qquad (7.32)$$

The rationale behind Equation (7.32) is straightforward. If the two intervals *do not* intersect, the *min* part in Equation (7.32) always generates a non-positive number and, therefore, $I(X, Y) = 0$. However, if the intervals intersect, the *min* part of the equation selects either $\overline{Y} - \underline{X} + \varepsilon$ or $\overline{X} - \underline{Y} + \varepsilon$ because $w(X)$ and $w(Y)$ are greater than or equal to either $\overline{Y} - \underline{X} + \varepsilon$ or $\overline{X} - \underline{Y} + \varepsilon$. Since either $\overline{Y} - \underline{X} + \varepsilon$ or $\overline{X} - \underline{Y} + \varepsilon$ is positive, maximizing with *0* yields the intersection width.

The rationale behind Equation (7.31) is not as straightforward. Given that the conclusion clause is true, we want to compute the truth of the given premise clause *and not vice versa*. In other words, we are trying to match the conclusion against the premise. This is reflected in Equation (7.31) by the denominator $w(C) + w(D)$. If, instead, we were to replace the denominator of Equation (7.31) by $w(A) + w(B)$, it would have meant that we are trying to match the premise against the conclusion. This, however, is incorrect because we cannot assume the truth of the premise without comparing it against the conclusion. To illustrate this point, consider the rule,

*If the distance is between 50 and 1000 m, Then the distance is far*

and assume that the user provides the data:

*The distance is 100 m*

Since $A = [50, 1000]$ and $C = [100, 100]$, whereas $B$ and $D$ are undefined, Equation (7.31) reduces to:

$$M = \frac{I(A,C)}{w(C)}$$

where $I(A, C) = \varepsilon$ and $w(C) = \varepsilon$, and yields the correct result $M = 1$. However, if we were to use $w(A) + w(B)$ instead of $w(C) + w(D)$ in the denominator of Equation (7.31), then this equation would be reduced to:

$$M = \frac{I(A,C)}{w(A)}$$

where $I(A, C) = \varepsilon$ and $w(A) = 950$, and would yield the incorrect result $M \approx 0$.

The role of $\varepsilon$ in calculating the width of an interval was already alluded to in Section 7.2.3 (see Equation (7.2)). It has to do with expressing numbers as intervals and it is of particular importance here in the context of the matching process. For example, if the premise of some rule is:

*John is 20*

and the conclusion of another rule is:

*John is 20*

then, since the clauses match perfectly, we expect that the matching process of Equation (7.31) would produce a matching factor $M = 1$.

To see that, note that each clause is associated with a singleton, namely, the premise clause is associated with $A = [20, 20]$ and the conclusion clause is associated with $C = [20, 20]$. The intervals $B$ and $D$ remain undefined. Hence, Equation (7.32) yields:

$$I(A,\ C) = max(0,\ min(w(A),w(C),\overline{C} - \underline{A} + \varepsilon, \overline{A} - \underline{C} + \varepsilon))$$

$$= max(0,\ \varepsilon)$$

$$= \varepsilon$$

Since $\varepsilon > 0$, then using Equation (7.31), we get:

$$M = \frac{I(A,C)}{w(C)} = \frac{\varepsilon}{20 - 20 + \varepsilon} = 1$$

as expected. Note that without $\varepsilon$, $M$ would have been indeterminate.

Let us change the example by changing the conclusion clause to:

*John is 21*

Now, since the two clauses do not match, we expect that the matching process of Equation (7.31) would produce a matching factor $M = 0$. Here, $A$ is still $[20, 20]$ but $C$ has changed to $[21, 21]$ and, therefore,

$$I(A,\ C) = max(0,\ min(w(A),w(C),\overline{C} - \underline{A} + \varepsilon, \overline{A} - \underline{C} + \varepsilon))$$

$$= max(0,\ -1 + \varepsilon)$$

$$= 0$$

since $\varepsilon > 0$ is arbitrarily small. Using Equation (7.31), we get:

$$M = \frac{I(A,C)}{w(C)} = \frac{0}{21 - 21 + \varepsilon} = 0$$

as expected. Again, note that without $\varepsilon$, $M$ would have been indeterminate.

The following examples further illustrate the use of Equation (7.31) to derive the matching factor $M$.

**Example 7.7:** Consider the following clauses:

*John is not more_or_less 20*

*John is almost 19*

Since the objects are the same (both clauses contain the object *John*), we can proceed to compute the matching factor between *not more_or_less 20* and *almost 19*.

Using the parsing procedure described in Section 7.2.2, we parse the two clauses and generate the intervals associated with them. Let $\alpha = 0$ and $\beta = 100$ be the lower and upper bounds, respectively, of the domain *OLD*. Assume that *more_or_less* generates the interval $[X-10\%,\ X+10\%]$, and *almost* generates the interval $[X-5\%,\ X-1\%]$, namely, *not more_or_less 20* $\Rightarrow$ *not* [18, 22] $\Rightarrow$ [0, 18–ε] and [22+ε, 100]

and

*almost 19* $\Rightarrow$ [18.05, 18.81]

Therefore, $A = [0, 18 - ε]$, $B = [22 + ε, 100]$, $C = [18.05, 18.81]$, and the interval $D$ remains undefined.

Hence, Equation (7.31) is reduced to:

$$M = \frac{I(A, C) + I(B, C)}{w(C)}$$

where,

$$I(A, C) = max(0, \ min(w(A), w(C), \overline{C} - \underline{A} + ε, \overline{A} - \underline{C} + ε))$$
$$= max(0, -0.05)$$
$$= 0$$

$$I(B, C) = max(0, \ min(w(B), w(C), \overline{C} - \underline{B} + ε, \overline{B} - \underline{C} + ε))$$
$$= max(0, -3.19)$$
$$= 0$$

and

$$w(C) = 0.76 + ε$$

Thus,

$$M = \frac{0}{0.76 + ε} = 0$$

namely, the two clauses *do not* match.

**Example 7.8:** Let the premise clause of some rule be:

*John is not 20 to 30*

and the conclusion clause of another rule be:

*John is 10 to 50*

If we assume that the domain of *OLD* is [0, 120], then parsing the conclusion clause creates the interval $C = [10, 50]$, and parsing the premise clause generates the dual interval $A = [0, 20–ε]$ and $B = [30+ε, 120]$. Again, the interval $D$ remains undefined.

Similarly to the previous example, Equation (7.31) is reduced to:

$$M = \frac{I(A,C) + I(B,C)}{w(C)}$$

where,

$$I(A,\ C) = max(0,\ min(w(A),w(C),\overline{C} - \underline{A} + \varepsilon, \overline{A} - \underline{C} + \varepsilon))$$
$$= max(0,\ 10)$$
$$= 0$$

$$I(B,\ C) = max(0,\ min(w(B),w(C),\overline{C} - \underline{B} + \varepsilon, \overline{B} - \underline{C} + \varepsilon))$$
$$= max(0,\ 20)$$
$$= 0$$

and

$$w(C) = 40 + \varepsilon$$

Thus, the degree to which the two clauses match is:

$$M = \frac{10 + 20}{40 + \varepsilon} \approx 0.75$$

It is instructive to review this result in terms of the given clauses. The conclusion of the rule becomes true (the rule fires) only if the premise is true (to a certain degree). The premise of the rule states that John's age is either *0 to 20* or *30 to 120* while the data states that John's age is *between 10 and 50*. Hence, if John's age is *between 0 and 20* or *between 30 and 120*, the rule will fire. However, it is also possible that John's age might be *between 20 and 30*, in which case the rule should not fire. These situations are reflected by the matching factor being less than one. Since the premise of the rule does not cover the possible range of the data, $M < 1$ indicates that the two clauses do not match exactly.

**Example 7.9:** Assume that the conclusion clause is associated with a single interval, $C = [70,\ 150]$, and that the parsed premise clause is also associated with a single interval, $A = [50,\ 100]$. Hence,

$$I(A,\ C) = max(0,\ min(w(A),w(C),\overline{C} - \underline{A} + \varepsilon, \overline{A} - \underline{C} + \varepsilon))$$
$$= max(0,\ 30 + \varepsilon)$$
$$= 30 + \varepsilon$$

and

$$w(C) = 80 + \varepsilon$$

and, therefore,

$$M = \frac{30 + \varepsilon}{80 + \varepsilon} \approx 0.375$$

To interpret this result, note that $I(A, C)$ and $w(C)$ imply that in 30 out of 80 possible cases the data match the premise of the rule. However, since the data contain a range that is not covered by the premise of the rule, the degree of belief that the conclusion of the rule is true is proportional to the degree to which the premise and the data match.

**Example 7.10:** Let the conclusion clause be associated with the singleton *70*, and assume that the premise clause is associated with interval [*50, 100*]. Similarly to Example 7.9, we have only two intervals, $C = [70, 70]$ and $A = [50, 100]$, however, in this case, $C$ is included in $A$. Hence,

$$I(A, C) = max(0, \ min(w(A), w(C), \overline{C} - \underline{A} + \varepsilon, \overline{A} - \underline{C} + \varepsilon))$$

$$= \varepsilon$$

and

$$w(C) = \varepsilon$$

and, therefore, $M = 1$.

Note that we have perfect matching between the premise and the conclusion because the data is in the range of the premise. In other words, it is not possible that the data will not be covered by all possible ranges of the rule.

**Example 7.11:** Let $A = [20, 30]$ and $C = [50, 80]$. Hence,

$$I(A, C) = max(0, \ min(w(A), w(C), \overline{C} - \underline{A} + \varepsilon, \overline{A} - \underline{C} + \varepsilon))$$

$$= max(0, \ -20 + \varepsilon)$$

$$= 0$$

and

$$w(C) = 30 + \varepsilon$$

so that,

$$M = \frac{0}{30 + \varepsilon} = 0$$

Clearly, since the two intervals do not intersect, they do not match.

**Example 7.12:** Let the conclusion clause be:

*Pressure is not 20 to 30*

and let the premise clause be:

*Pressure is not 35 to 45*

and assume that the domain of *Pressure* is $[0, 100]$. Parsing the two clauses yields $A = [0, 35-\varepsilon]$, $B = [45+\varepsilon, 100]$, $C = [0, 20-\varepsilon]$, and $D = [30+\varepsilon, 100]$. Thus,

$$I(A, C) = max(0, \ min(w(A), w(C), \overline{C} - \underline{A} + \varepsilon, \overline{A} - \underline{C} + \varepsilon))$$
$$= 20$$

$$I(A, D) = max(0, \ min(w(A), w(D), \overline{D} - \underline{A} + \varepsilon, \overline{A} - \underline{D} + \varepsilon))$$
$$= 5 - \varepsilon$$

$$I(B, C) = max(0, \ min(w(B), w(C), \overline{C} - \underline{B} + \varepsilon, \overline{B} - \underline{C} + \varepsilon))$$
$$= 0$$

$$I(B, D) = max(0, \ min(w(B), w(D), \overline{D} - \underline{B} + \varepsilon, \overline{B} - \underline{D} + \varepsilon))$$
$$= 55$$

and

$$w(C) \ = \ 20$$
$$w(D) \ = \ 70$$

Substituting these results into Equation (7.31) yields:

$$M = \frac{80 - \varepsilon}{90} \approx 0.88$$

## 7.3.3 Matching Regular Clauses With Mathematical Clauses

Mathematical clauses have two forms: (i) an *assignment statement* if the mathematical clause is in the conclusion part of the rule, and (ii) a *logical expression* if the mathematical clause is in the premise of the rule. Let us, therefore, consider the matching process between regular clauses without fuzzy variables and mathematical clauses in accordance with this distinction.

1.  *Assignment statement.* Let the regular clause $R_c^{\overline{M}}$ be

    $$X \ is \ Y$$

    and let the mathematical clause $M_C$ be in the form of an *assignment statement*:

    $$[X^* := expression]$$

    Clearly, if $X$ and $X^*$ do not match, then the two clauses do not match. However, assuming that $X$ and $X^*$ match, then we have to consider the following two cases.

    (i) If both clauses can be evaluated during preprocessing, namely, the values of all the variables in the *expression* are known and $Y$ is not a word, then:

$$MF = M \quad if\ X = X^*$$

or
(7.33a)

$$MF = M \quad if\ X \neq X^*$$

and

$$MG = -2 \tag{7.33b}$$

Note that $MG$ is set to $-2$ since the regular clause is not associated with a membership function.

**Example 7.13:** Consider the following clauses:

*Pressure is 55 to 65*

*[Pressure := 60]*

Since $X = X^*$, we use Equation (7.31) to calculate the matching factor. The result $M = 1$ sets $MF = 1$ and, since the regular clause is $R_c^{\overline{M}}$, we set $MG = -2$.

(ii) If one of the clauses cannot be evaluated during preprocessing, then:

$$MF = \begin{cases} 0 & if\ X \neq X^* \\ -1 & if\ X = X^* \end{cases} \tag{7.34a}$$

$$MG = -2 \tag{7.34b}$$

Recall that $MF = -1$ indicates that there is a *potential* link between the two clauses (see Equation (7.26)), but that it can be determined only during inferencing. Here, too, the parameter $MG$ is set to $-2$ in accordance with Equation (7.25).

**Example 7.14:** Let the two clauses be:

*Pressure is 50*

*[Pressure := Z]*

Since $X = X^*$, the value of *Pressure* cannot be evaluated during pre-processing. Hence, we set $MF = -1$, and since *50* is not a fuzzy variable, we set $MG = -2$.

2.  *Logical expression.* Let the regular clause $R_c^{\overline{M}}$ be

*X is Y*

and let the mathematical clause $M_c$ be a *logical expression* in the form of:

$$[\xi < op > \eta]$$

where $\xi$ and $\eta$ are two expressions and $< op >$ denotes any logical relation among them.

Since the logical expression always contains at least one variable whose value is unknown during preprocessing, the parameters $MF$ and $MG$ are computed as follows:

$$MF = \begin{cases} 0 & \text{if } X \notin \xi, \eta \\ -1 & \text{if } X \in \xi, \eta \end{cases} \qquad (7.35a)$$

and

$$MG = -2 \qquad (7.35b)$$

**Example 7.15:** Let the two clauses be

*Pressure is 20*

*[Pressure := Z]*

Since $Z$ is a variable whose value is unknown during preprocessing, we set $MF$ to $-1$. We set $MG = -2$ because the clauses are not associated with membership functions.

### 7.3.4 Matching Executable Clauses With Any Clause

Since the executable clause $E_C$ is a call to perform a task, it cannot be matched with any other type of clause. Hence, letting $C$ be some clause, then:

$$MF = \quad 0 \;\; if\, C \;\; is \;\; E_C \qquad (7.36a)$$

$$MG = -2 \;\; if\, C \;\; is \;\; E_C \qquad (7.36b)$$

**Example 7.16:** Consider the clauses:

*{recognize object_1}*

*object_1 is recognized*

It is clear that the first clause is a call to the procedure *recognize object_1* while the second clause is a regular clause that has to be matched to another non-executable clause. Since there is no link between the two clauses, we set the $MF=0$ and $MG=-2$.

### 7.3.5 Matching Fuzzy Clauses With Fuzzy Clauses

When we match two $R_c^M$ clauses (namely, regular clauses that are associated with membership functions), the only case we have to consider is that of identical clauses in both object and subject. Hence, if the two clauses are:

$$c\_1: X \text{ is } Y$$

and

$$c\_2: X^* \text{ is } Y^*$$

then

$$M = \begin{cases} 1 & \text{if } X = X^* \text{and } Y = Y^* \\ 0 & \text{otherwise} \end{cases} \qquad (7.37a)$$

and, therefore, $MF$ is also either $1$ or $0$, and

$$MG = \begin{cases} -1 & \text{if } X = X^* \text{and } Y = Y^* \\ -2 & \text{otherwise} \end{cases} \qquad (7.37b)$$

In other words, we have a perfect match, $M = 1$, if the clauses are identical, and no match otherwise. We assign $MG = -1$ when the two clauses are identical because the actual membership grades can be determined *only* during run time.

**Example 7.17:** If both clauses have the same form, namely, $X$ is $Y$, then regardless of the fact that $Y$ is a fuzzy variable, we match the clauses using the algorithm described in Section 7.3.2. For example, assume the following two clauses:

*Pressure is high*

*Pressure is high*

It is clear that the clauses match and the fact that *high_pressure* is a fuzzy variable is .irrelevant. However, because we do not know during preprocessing how high the pressure is, we set the value of the $MG$ to $-1$ to indicate that the *actual* membership grade will be computed during the inference process. The matching factor $MF$ is set to $1$ because there is an *exact* match between the clauses.

### 7.3.6 Matching Fuzzy Clauses With Regular Clauses

When we match two clauses only one of which is associated with a membership function, we have to consider several cases. Let the clause associated with the membership function $R_c^M$ be

$$c\_1: X \text{ is } Y$$

and let the other clause $R_c^{\overline{M}}$ be

$$c\_2: X^* \text{ is } Y^*$$

Since $Y$ is associated with a membership function, it must be a *word*. On the other hand, $Y^*$ can be a *word*, a *number*, an *interval*, or a *dual interval* (see Section 7.2.2). Let us consider these cases assuming that $X = X^*$.

1.  *Y\* is a word.* If $Y = Y^*$, we have the same case as in Section 7.3.1. Otherwise, if $Y \neq Y^*$, then the clauses do not match.

2.  *Y\* is a number.* Here we can compute the membership grade of $Y^*$ in the fuzzy set associated with $Y$ and, therefore, we must also account for cases in which $Y$ is modified and/or negated.

    * $c_1$: *X is Y.* The two parameters $MF$ and $MG$ are determined in this case as follows:

$$M = \begin{cases} 1 & \text{if } X = X^* \text{ and } MG = -2 \\ 0 & \text{otherwise} \end{cases} \qquad (7.37a)$$

and, therefore, $MF$ is also either *1* or *0*, and

$$MG = \chi_Y(Y^*) \qquad (7.38b)$$

**Example 7.18:** Consider the following clauses:

> *Pressure is high*
>
> *Pressure is 60*

Assume that the domain of *pressure* is *[0, 120]* with the membership function *S(40, 70, 100)* (see Equation (3.1)). Since the subjects of the two clauses match, we apply the number *60* to the membership function *S(40, 70, 100)* and get:

$$\chi_{high\_pressure}(60) = 0.22$$

The matching factor $MF$ is set to *1* because there is a match ($M = 1$) between the two clauses.

* $c_1$: *X is MOD Y.* The parameter $MF$ is determined by Equation (7.26) but we have to update the parameter $MG$ to take into account the intensity $V$ associated with the *local* modifier[1]. Hence,

$$MG = \chi_Y(Y^*) \cdot V \qquad (7.39)$$

For example, consider the clauses:

> *Pressure is almost high*
>
> *Pressure is 60*

---

[1] A *local* modifier is a regular modifier as described in Section 7.2.2, however, it is treated differently. If $Y$ is a number in a clause which is not associated with a membership function, then the modifier creates an interval. If the modifier is associated with a membership function, then it intensifies $Y$.

Let the domain of *pressure* and the membership function associated with the variable *pressure* be the same as in Example 7.18, and let the local modifier *almost* be associated with $V = 0.8$. Hence:

$$MG = \chi_{high\_pressure}(60)V = 0.22 \times 0.8 = 0.176$$

- $c_1$: *X is NOT Y.* The parameter $MF$ is determined by Equation (7.26) whereas the parameter $MG$ is modified to read:

$$MG = 1 - \chi_Y(Y^*) \tag{7.40}$$

Note that the negation operator is different here. When *NOT* is associated with a membership function, then it is treated as in Equation (7.40), whereas when the *NOT* operator is not associated with a membership function, then it is treated as in Section 7.2.2.

For example, given the clauses:

*Pressure is not high*

*Pressure is 60*

we obtain:

$$MG = 1 - \chi_{high\_pressure}(60) = 1 - 0.22 = 0.78$$

- $c_1$: *X is NOT MOD Y.* Here, too, the parameter $MF$ is unchanged but the parameter $MG$ is updated to:

$$MG = 1 - \chi_Y(Y^*) \cdot V \tag{7.41}$$

To illustrate this, consider the clauses:

*Pressure is not almost high*

*Pressure is 60*

and let the local modifier *almost* be associated with $V = 0.8$. Hence:

$$MG = 1 - \chi_{high\_pressure}(60)V = 1 - 0.22 \times 0.8 = 0.824$$

3. *$Y^*$ is an interval.* The clause $R_c^{\overline{M}}$ in this case is in the form:

$$c_2: X^* \text{ is } [N1, N2]$$

We can transform this case into the previous Case 2 by letting $N$ be the midpoint of $N1$ and $N2$, $N = \frac{1}{2}(N1 + N2)$, and rewriting $c_2$ as:

$$c_2: X^* \text{ is } N$$

4. *$Y^*$ is a dual interval.* Since $X = X^*$, we know that there is a link between the two clauses, however, we do not know its value during preprocessing. Therefore, we set both $MF$ and $MG$ to $-1$.

### 7.3.7 Matching Fuzzy Clauses With Mathematical Clauses

Following Section 7.3.3, we divide the discussion of matching regular clauses *with* fuzzy variables with mathematical clauses according to the form taken by the mathematical clause: an assignment statement or a logical relation.

1.  Let the fuzzy regular clause $R_c^M$ be:

$$X \text{ is } Y$$

and let the mathematical clause $M_C$ be in the form of *assignment statement*:

$$[X^* := expression]$$

Clearly, if $X$ and $X^*$ do not match, then the clauses do not match. However, assuming that $X$ and $X^*$ match[2], then we have to consider the following two cases.

(i) If $X^*$ can be evaluated during preprocessing, then

$$MG = \begin{cases} \chi_Y(X^*) & \text{if } X = X^* \\ -2 & \text{otherwise} \end{cases} \tag{7.42}$$

whereas $MF$ is set according to Equation (7.26).

**Example 7.19:** Consider the clauses:

$$Pressure \text{ is high}$$

$$[Pressure := 60]$$

and assume that *high_pressure* is associated with the membership function *SIG(30, 50, 70)* (see Equation (3.1)). Since $X = X^*$, we set $MG = \chi_{high\_pressure}(60) = 0.88$. Furthermore, since the matching between the two clauses can be evaluated during preprocessing and since it is, in this case, a perfect match, $M = 1$, we set $MF = 1$ according to Equation (7.26).

(ii) If $X^*$ cannot be evaluated during preprocessing, then:

$$MG = \begin{cases} -1 & \text{if } X = X^* \\ -2 & \text{otherwise} \end{cases} \tag{7.43}$$

Note that $MG = -1$ indicates that there is a potential link between the two clauses provided that $X^*$ will be evaluated during inferencing. The parameter $MF$ is set to $-1$ according to Equation (7.26).

**Example 7.20:** Let the two clauses be

$$Pressure \text{ is high}$$

---

[2] $X$ and $X^*$ match $\Rightarrow X = X^* \Leftrightarrow X$ and $X^*$ are identical or synonymical.

$$[Pressure := Z]$$

where $R_c^M$ is associated with the fuzzy set *high_pressure*. As we can see, there is a potential link between the clauses. Therefore, we set $MG = -1$ and $MF = -1$.

2.   Let the fuzzy regular clause $R_c^M$ be in the form

$$X \; is \; Y$$

and let the mathematical clause $M_C$ be in the form of a *logical expression*:

$$[e_1 < op > e_2]$$

where $e_1$ and $e_2$ are two expressions and $< op >$ denotes any logical relation among them. If the logical expression contains at least one variable, it cannot be evaluated during preprocessing, and we have:

$$MF = \begin{cases} 0 & if \; X \notin e_1, e_2 \\ -1 & if \; X \in e_1, e_2 \end{cases} \qquad (7.44a)$$

and

$$MG = \begin{cases} -1 & if \; X \in e_1, e_2 \\ -2 & otherwise \end{cases} \qquad (7.44b)$$

**Example 7.21:** Consider the clauses:

$$Pressure \; is \; high$$

$$[Pressure := 20]$$

Since *pressure* is a variable whose value will be known *only* in the inference process, we set $MF = -1$ and $MG = -1$.

### 7.3.8  Adding Relations To The Relational List

Using Equations (7.25) and (7.26), we create the *relational list* (R-list) which contains the relations among the rules in the knowledge base. The construction of the R-list is quite simple: we compare each conclusion clause with all the premise clauses. Hence, if

$$M(conclusion \; clause, premise \; clause) \geq T \qquad (7.45)$$

where $T$ is some threshold, then we add that relation to the R-list.

Both the R-list and the $W_{R_n}$ (see Equation (7.1)) are stored permanently, and will not be changed unless the user alters the knowledge base.

# 8 KNOWLEDGE IN FEST

*FEST*'s main menu consisting of four items was introduced in Chapter 2. The four main menu items, shown in Figure 2.1, are:

1. *File*

2. *Grammar*

3. *ES-Shell*

4. *Quit*

*Quit* was considered in Chapter 2 and the details of *ES-Shell* will be discussed in Chapter 11. In this chapter, we introduce the first and second menu items. We begin with *Grammar* and continue with *File*.

## 8.1 Grammar

Knowledge representation refers to the structures used to represent knowledge in the expert system. Efficient knowledge representation is the key to the successful implementation of the expert system. Through the use of an appropriate representation, knowledge can be manipulated effectively and precisely so that the expert system can arrive at the correct conclusions.

*FEST*'s *Grammar* option provides the capability to create and/or modify the knowledge structures of knowledge bases. This capability allows the expert system shell to process knowledge bases with different structures, thereby increasing the adaptability and processing power of the expert system.

Usually, a new grammar (or structure) is created when different knowledge bases with different structures need to be incorporated within the same expert system shell. To create a new grammar, *FEST* must be provided with an example. The power of the newly created grammar depends on the extent and complexity of the example.

We can modify knowledge by modifying the content of the rule base (e.g., add, delete, or modify existing rules in the given knowledge base) as we will show later (see *Edit KB* in Section 8.2), or we can modify the structure (grammar) of the knowledge base itself. Since the knowledge structure for any application may change over time, the need for a modifiable structure becomes apparent, and is addressed in this section.

We consider two approaches to knowledge structure modification. First, we can modify the lexicon or the grammar through simple knowledge acquisition. Second, we can modify the transition table associated with the given grammar.

Recall that the *Grammar* menu, shown in Figure 2.3 of Chapter 2, consists of the following four items.

1.  *Test Expression*: Allows us to test the validity of a rule and to learn about the grammar of the knowledge base

2.  *Transition Table*: Modifies the grammar

3.  *Modify Lexicon*: Modifies the lexicon of the grammar

4.  *Create Grammar*: Allows us to create a new grammar

In the following sections, we describe these options in detail and show how to modify the various parts of the grammar, or how to create a new grammar.


### 8.1.1  Test Expression

The *Test Expression* menu item enables us to check the grammatical consistency of the entered expression according to the rules of the grammar currently used by the parser. It is a useful tool that allows new users as well as experienced knowledge engineers to practice and learn about the grammar of the knowledge base. In any case, if the grammar does not suit your needs, you can use the option of modifying the grammar.

As was mentioned earlier, *FEST* must be provided with an example. Thus, upon entering a sample rule, *FEST* attempts to parse it and generates an error message if the rule does not comply with the rules of the grammar currently in use. In this case, when the structure of the entered rule contradicts the grammar, we can either correct it in accordance with the displayed error message, or abandon it by pressing the **ESC** key. On the other hand, if the sample rule is grammatically correct, *FEST* displays the transition table (see Section 8.1.2) associated with that rule.

To illustrate this process, let us consider the example shown in Figure 8.1. Upon selecting *Test Expression, FEST* opens a window where we enter the following rule:

*If the colour of the house is not more_or_less Then the colour of the house is blue*

Attempting to parse this rule, *FEST* generates the error message:

*Expected IDENTIFIER or INTEGER or REAL, found THEN*

which means that the parser was expecting an object (*IDENTIFIER*), an integer, or a real number, but found instead the keyword *THEN*. Pressing the **ENTER** key, *FEST* invokes the editor, puts the cursor in the suspected place, and lets us correct the error. In the above example, we can correct the error by placing some identifier (word) in front of the keyword *THEN*, e.g. the word *GREEN*.

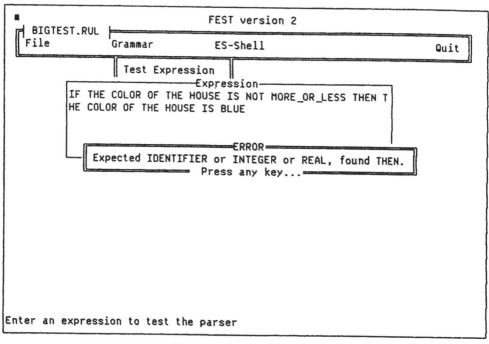

**Figure 8.1** Testing a rule

After correcting the error(s), *FEST* attempts to parse the rule again. This process continues until the rule is accepted by the grammar. (Note that we can terminate the process at any time by pressing the **ESC** key.) At this point, *FEST* displays the *transition table* of the *finite state machine* that corresponds to the parsing process, as shown in Figure 8.2.

The four columns of the transition table in Figure 8.2 specify the finite state machine as follows.

Column 1 - *Present*: Shows the present state.

Column 2 - *Token*: Indicates the set to which the token's symbol belongs (e.g. *identifiers, verbs, prepositions, articles, modifiers, special words and characters*, etc.).

Column 3 - *Symbol*: Specifies the token type.

Column 4 - *Next*: Shows the next state.

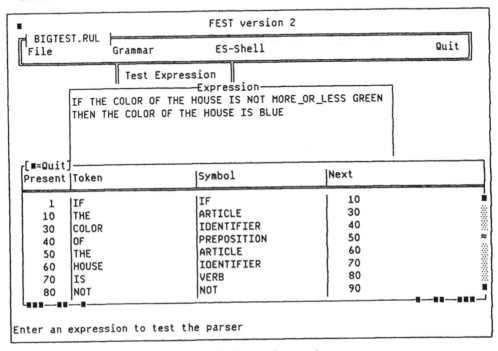

**Figure 8.2** Correcting a rule

## 8.1.2 Transition Table

This menu item allows us to modify the current grammar by editing the *finite state machine* which is the tool used to represent grammars in *FEST*. Choosing this option, the window shown in Figure 8.3 displays the *transition table* of *FEST*'s general grammar, which is now in the form of a 3-tuple list that represents the relations among states.

The three columns of the transition table in Figure 8.3 specify the finite state machine as follows.

Column 1 - *Present*: Shows the present state.

Column 2 - *Symbol*: Specifies the token type.

Column 3 - *Next*: Shows the next state.

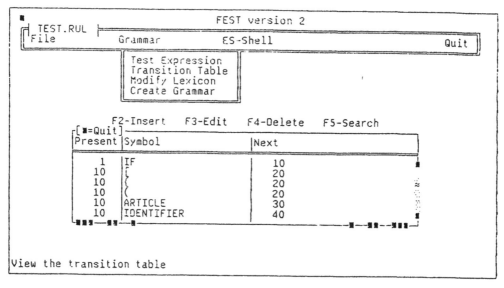

**Figure 8.3** Transition table

The interpretation of the transition table is very simple. Each row in the table indicates the type of input symbol required for a transition from the present state to the next state. For example, consider the row

*10 ARTICLE 30*

where *10* and *30* designate the present and next states, respectively, and *ARTICLE* stands for the input symbol. Thus, when the parser sees an article, it moves from state *10* to state *30*. However, if in some present state the parser encounters a symbol different from the one indicated by that row of the transition table, it will not be able to move to the next state and will output an error message instead.

To edit the transition table, we can utilize the following function keys.

- **F2-Insert:** This function key allows us to add (insert) new states to the transition table, or to add new transitions to existing ones.

    For example, we can add the line

*90 IDENTIFIER 120*

to the transition table to tell the parser to move from the present state *90* to the next state *120* with the input being an identifier. If we now add

*120 EOL_SYM 000*

where *EOL* stands for end-of-line, we insert a new state to the transition table, indicating to the parser that the identifier symbol may be the last token (word) in the rule. These two examples are shown below in graphical form.

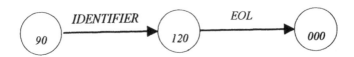

To avoid errors, you can review the list of all possible legal symbols prior to adding a new line to the transition table or modifying an input symbol. To do so, press the **ENTER** key to display the list of legal symbols when you are asked to enter the token (symbol) name. You can then choose a symbol from the list, and pressing the **ENTER** key, that symbol will be inserted into the transition table.

- **F3-Edit:** This function key allows us to modify existing relations in the transition table. To do so, we move the cursor to the appropriate line and column and then press **F3** to invoke the editor which will prompt us to make the modification.

    Similarly to **F2**, we can review the list of all possible legal symbols by pressing the **ENTER** key to display the list of legal symbols.

- **F4-Delete:** With this function key we can delete a line (or a record) from the transition table. Note, however, that a line (or a record) is permanently deleted *only* when we exit *FEST*. As long as we do not exit *FEST*, the line (or record) is marked to indicate to the grammar that it should not consider that line (or record) when parsing the rule. Thus, if for some reason or another we decide to undelete a deleted line, we have the option to do so.

    To delete a line (or record), place the cursor on the desired line (or record) and press **F4**. The color of the selected line changes to indicate that the line is deleted as far as the grammar is concerned; however, since it is not really deleted, it remains displayed in the window. To undelete a line, locate the line and press **F4** key.

- **F5-Search:** With this function key we can search the transition table for a particular state or token.

To move about the transition table, we can use the four arrow keys and the *Home, End, PgUp* (page up), and *PgDn* (page down) keys. These keys are listed in Table 8.1.

As we can see, *FEST* provides a very powerful tool for modifying the grammar to fit specific applications. However, since the inference engine of *FEST* has specific instructions on how to handle the grammar, we should be very careful in modifying it. Caution should be exercised by taking into account the following.

- The inference engine can handle up to four identifiers whereas the grammar allows us to define as many identifiers as we may wish to. However, *FEST*'s inference engine will use *only* the first four identifiers.

**Table 8.1** Transition table keys

| | |
|---|---|
| ← | Moves the cursor one field (column) to the left |
| → | Moves the cursor one field (column) to the right |
| ↑ | Moves the cursor one line (record) up |
| ↓ | Moves the cursor one line (record) down |
| *Home* | Positions the cursor at the first column of the first line |
| *End* | Positions the cursor at the first column of the last line |
| *PgUp* | Moves the cursor one page up |
| *PgDn* | Moves the cursor one page down |

- The inference engine can handle up to two bounding intervals (four bounds) on the object that result from processing clauses without fuzzy variables (see Section 7.2.2).

  For example, *FEST* can handle the clauses *pressure is 20 to 30*, whose corresponding bounding interval is *[20, 30]* whereas the second bounding interval is undefined, and *pressure is 20 to 30 or 50 to 60*, whose corresponding the bounding intervals are *[20, 30]* and *[50, 60]*. However, if we change the clause to *pressure is 20 to 30 or 50 to 60 or 80 to 100*, whose bounding intervals are *[20, 30]*, *[50, 60]*, and *[80, 100]*, *FEST* will use *only* the first two intervals and ignore the third. Note that in order to deal with this kind of clause, we would have to break it into two clauses.

- *FEST* can handle *only* one modifier per clause.

When we want to create a new knowledge base (see *Create* in Section 8.2.1), *FEST* loads the default grammar, which is the most complete grammar that can be generated based on the restrictions described above. In some cases, however, we may not need such complicated grammar and, therefore, we have the option of modifying it. Nevertheless, having a default grammar enables us to use the same shell with different knowledge bases, where each knowledge base may have a different grammar.

## 8.1.3 Lexicon Modification

The lexicon is the vocabulary (or dictionary) of the expert system. *FEST* allows us to modify the lexicon of a given grammar through knowledge acquisition, thus adding power and flexibility to the construction of the knowledge base.

The lexicon consists of the four elements shown in Figure 8.4, each of which can be edited using the editor function keys introduced in Section 8.1.2.

1.  *Articles:* Insert, delete, edit, or search for articles in the article list associated with the grammar. The default set of the articles includes the articles *an, the, a, this, these, those, that,* and *they.*

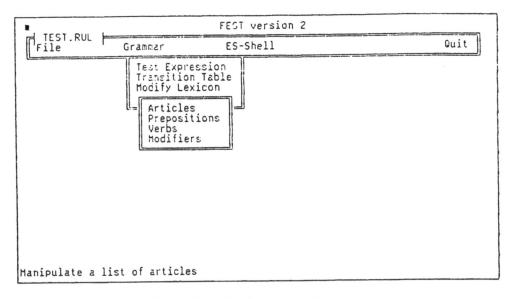

**Figure 8.4** Modify lexicon submenu

2.  *Prepositions:* Allow us to insert, delete, edit, or search for prepositions in the preposition list associated with the grammar. The default set of the prepositions include the prepositions *on, in, about, around, at, by, for, near of, through, above, below, under,* and *beside.*

3.  *Verbs:* We can insert, delete, edit, or search for verbs in the verb list associated with the grammar. The default set of the verbs include the verbs *be, is, are, am, was,* etc.

4.  *Modifiers:* Allow us to insert, delete, edit, or search for modifiers in the modifier list associated with the grammar. Examples of modifiers are *more_or_less, almost, more_than,* etc. Recall that each modifier is associated with some lower bound and upper bound that are used to generate the object's bounding intervals (see Section 7.2).

    Note that whenever a modifier is modified, it affects the entire knowledge base. This means that when a modifier is being changed, *FEST* re-evaluates all the clauses that use the changed modifier, as well as the relational list.

### 8.1.4 Create Grammar

To define a new grammar, we have to provide *FEST* with an example of a rule. Based on this exemplar, *FEST* generates a parsable grammar as shown in Figure 8.5. Upon completing this process, *FEST* displays the new transition table, prompts us to confirm it, and then deletes the old grammar (the default grammar) so that the new grammar becomes the grammar used by the parser.

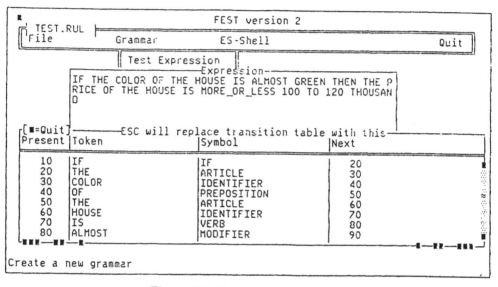

**Figure 8.5** Creating new grammar

## 8.2 File

The *File* option, introduced in Chapter 2 and depicted in Figure 2.2, consists of four items:

- *K-Base*
- *Synonym*
- *M-Function*
- *DOS*

We have already described the *DOS* option in Chapter 2. In this section, we consider the remaining options, namely, *K-Base*, *Synonym*, and *M-Function*.

### 8.2.1 K-Base

The *K-Base* menu consists of the following ten functions.

1.  *Load:* Links an existing knowledge base with *FEST*. Selecting this option, we are provided with a list of all the available knowledge bases and can use the keyboard or the mouse to choose the desired knowledge base. Upon choosing a knowledge base, *FEST* loads the knowledge base with its associated files.

2.  *Create:* This option allows us to create a new knowledge base. When we invoke *Create, FEST* asks us to name the knowledge base and opens all the necessary files and data structures into which we can insert the rules.

3.  *Generate:* Rebuilds the relational list of the currently-used knowledge base.

4.  *Delete KB:* This option enables us to delete knowledge bases which are no longer useful, are out-dated, or are erroneous. While we can remove them through the DOS environment, it is preferable to do so through *FEST* because, in this case, all the index files will also be removed.

    When we invoke this option, *FEST* displays the list of all the existing knowledge bases (as in *Load*). Selecting a knowledge base and pressing the **ENTER** key, the knowledge base will be deleted after confirmation.

5.  *Import KB:* We can prepare a knowledge base in text format outside the *FEST* environment and then use the *Import KB* option to let *FEST* generate the knowledge base by parsing every rule, creating the proper data structures, and placing the proper knowledge in the proper data structures.

    This option is also very useful in automatic knowledge generation. We may have a device that creates the knowledge base and then passes it to *FEST* for proper parsing and generation [103, 104, 105].

6.  *Export KB:* Generates an ASCII file of the currently-used knowledge base. We can edit this file externally and then import it into *FEST* using the *Import KB* option.

7.  *Print KB:* With this option we can print the currently-used knowledge base or some of its associated files using the following printing selection:

    - *Print Rules* - prints the rules and their associated weights
    - *Print Premise* - prints the premise parts of the rules
    - *Print Conc* - prints the conclusion parts of the rules
    - *Print R-list* - prints the relational list
    - *Print Member* - prints the membership functions
    - *Print Grammar* - prints the transition table.

8.  *Edit K-Base:* Allows us to view a knowledge base or to modify it. As shown in Figure 8.6, *Edit K-Base* invokes two windows, the main editor window and a rule display window.

```
■                              FEST version 2
 ┌┤TEST.RUL├──────────────────────────────────────────────────
 ║'File          Grammar          ES-Shell              Quit  ║
  ║┌ K-Base ─────┤│
  ║║             ║  F2-Insert    F3-Edit    F4-Delete   F5-Search
 ┌[■=Quit]────────────────────────────────────────────────────
 │No.│Rule (... truncated)                │Priority│Conf.│Conc.│Weight
 ├───────────────────────────────────────────────────────────
 │ 1│IF M IS M THEN Y IS Y                │1.00   │1.00 │ 1.00│1.00  ■
 │ 2│IF W IS W AND X IS X THEN   ...      │1.00   │1.00 │ 1.00│1.00
 │ 3│IF AA IS AA AND B IS B THE ...       │1.00   │1.00 │ 1.00│1.00
 │ 4│IF D IS D OR Z IS Z THEN E ...       │1.00   │1.00 │ 1.00│1.00
 │ 5│IF C IS C AND E IS E THEN   ...      │1.00   │1.00 │ 1.00│1.00
 │ 6│IF X IS X THEN AA IS AA              │1.00   │1.00 │ 1.00│1.00
 │ 7│IF Y IS Y THEN B IS B                │1.00   │1.00 │ 1.00│1.00
 │ 8│IF F IS F THEN S IS S                │1.00   │1.00 │ 1.00│1.00
 │ 9│IF G IS G THEN R IS R                │1.00   │1.00 │ 1.00│1.00  ■
 └■■■──■■──■─────────────────────────────────────────────■──■■──■■■─┘
                          ─Full Rule─
 │IF M IS M THEN Y IS Y                                        │

 F1-Help │ Edit the rules of the currently loaded knowledge base
```

**Figure 8.6** Editing knowledge base

The rule display window displays the highlighted rule in its entirety whereas the main editor window is divided into six columns.

Column1: *Rule number* - this number is generated by *FEST* and is used for reference in the editing, displaying, and inferencing modes.

Column 2: *Truncated description of the rule* - if the rule is too long, this field displays a truncated version of the rule. Nevertheless, the entire rule is shown in the rule display window.

Column 3: *The rule's priority RP* (see Section 7.1).

Column 4: *The rule's confidence or certainty RC* (see Section 7.1).

Column 5: *The rule's conclusion certainty CC* (see Sections 6.2 and 10.1.4).

Column 6: *The overall weight of the rule $W_{R_i}$* (see Equation (7.1)).

We can modify the rule and its associated uncertainties (Columns 2 - 5) by moving the cursor in the main editor window to the appropriate row and column and pressing **F3-Edit**. If we want to add or delete a rule, we use the keys **F2-Insert** and **F4-Delete**, respectively. To search the knowledge base, we can use the key **F5-Search**.

9. *Options:* Allows us to change the values of the following default parameters.

- *Priority Wgt* - the weight $W_{RP}$ of the rule's priority $RP$ whose default value is 1 (see Section 7.1).
- *Certainty Wgt* - the weight $W_{RC}$ of the rule's certainty $RC$ whose default value is 1 (see Section 7.1).
- *Threshold* - the threshold whose default value is 0.5. The threshold is used to determine whether a rule would be fired or not.
- *M-Func Partition* - defines the number of quantization levels of the domain of the membership function. Increasing this number will tend to improve the accuracy of the inverse membership grade, $\chi^{-1}$, in the defuzzification process (see Section 10.2.1). The default value of this parameter is 20.
- *Mbr Tolerance* - the difference between the estimated $\chi^{-1}$ obtained through inferencing and the $\chi^{-1}$ obtained via the quantization levels of the domain. The default value of this parameter is 0.0050.
- *Epsilon* - the $\varepsilon$ whose default value is 0.000100 (see Equation (7.2)).
- *Printer Port* - the default printer port is 1.
- *Multiple Conclusions* - turning this parameter off would terminate the inferencing when *FEST* reaches the first conclusion. The default value of this parameter is $Y$ (on).
- *Check Synonyms* - turning this parameter off instructs instructing *FEST* not to check for synonyms. The default value of this parameter is $Y$ (on).

10. *Display:* Enables us to display all the files and data structures associated with a given knowledge base. We have four options when we invoke *Display*.

- *Knowledge Base* - displays the knowledge base similarly to Figure 8.6 but without the editing facilities.
- *Premise File* - displays the parsed form of the premise (antecedent) part of every rule as shown in Figure 8.7. The window is divided into the following columns.

    1. *R/NO*: The rule number associated with the clause.
    2. *C/NO*: Since each premise may contain a number of different clauses, this column indicates the clause number. The clause and rule numbers are very important for the inferencing process because they uniquely identify each type of clause.
    3. *C/TYPE*: In *FEST*, we distinguish between four types of clauses (see Chapter 7):

       *Type 0*: Designates regular English clause (as described earlier).

> *Type 1:* Designates logical operators such as *AND* and *OR*.
>
> *Type 2:* Designates a mathematical expression.
>
> *Type 3:* Designates an executable function.

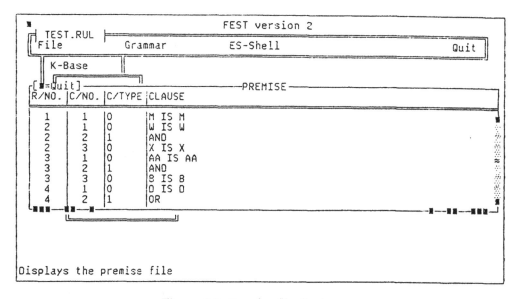

```
■                                          FEST version 2
┌─┐ TEST.RUL  ├════════════════════════════════════════════════════┐
│├'File          Grammar            ES-Shell                      Quit │
│└─────────────────────────────────────────────────────────────────┘
│  ┌──────────────┐
│  │  K-Base      │
│  └──────────────┘
│ ┌[■=Quit]──────────────────────────────PREMISE────────────────────
│ │R/NO. │C/NO. │C/TYPE │CLAUSE
│ │
│     1      1      0     │M IS M
│     2      1      0     │W IS W                                      ■
│     2      2      1     │AND
│     2      3      0     │X IS X
│     3      1      0     │AA IS AA                                    ≈
│     3      2      1     │AND
│     3      3      0     │B IS B
│     4      1      0     │D IS D
│     4      2      1     │OR                                          ■
│ └■■■──■■─■───────────────────────────────────────────────■──■■─■■■─┘
│        └─────────────────────────────────┘
│
│
│Displays the premise file
└──────────────────────────────────────────────────────────────────┘
```

**Figure 8.7**  Premise file display

4. *CLAUSE:* Displays the clause itself.

5. *OBJECT1 - OBJECT4:* Four fields that display the four identifiers (see Section 8.1.2).

6. *MODIFIER:* Displays the modifiers (recall that *FEST* accepts only one modifier per clause).

7. *NOTUSED:* Boolean field that indicates whether or not the *NOT* operator is used in the clause.

8. *MATCH:* This field is not used in *FEST*.

9. *NUMBER1 - NUMBER4:* Four fields that display the four bounds on the object's clause (see Section 8.1.2).

• *Conclusion File* - displays the parsed form of the conclusion part of every rule similarly to the display of the premise file.

• *R-list File* - displays the relational list that depicts the relations among the clauses within the given knowledge base. The window is divided into the following columns:

1. *C-Rule*: A rule number

2. *C-Clause*: The clause number in *C-Rule*

3. *P-Rule*: Another rule number

4. *P-Clause*: The clause number in *P-Rule*

5. *Match Value*: The degree of similarity, *MF*, between the two clauses (*C-Clause* and *P-Clause*) (see Section 7.3).

6. *Mbr Value*: The degree of membership, *MG*, of *C-Clause* with respect to *P-Clause*(see Section 7.3).

## 8.2.2 Synonym

This menu item enables us to associate up to five different synonyms with each keyword. Thus, we can define rules with different notations and yet the inference engine is able to infer on them using the keywords list.

For example, consider the following two rules:

*If people are hungry Then provide food*

*If there is no money Then men are hungry*

In a conventional expert system, the inference engine would not be able to link these rules because *people* and *men* are two different words, and therefore it would not be able to make any inference. However, in *FEST*, the synonym option allows us to make these two words synonymous. Therefore, *FEST* can link the conclusion of the second rule to the premise of the first rule and conclude that *people are hungry* and *men are hungry* have the same meaning.

The process of inserting new synonyms or keywords, editing them, deleting synonyms or keywords, or simply searching for certain information in the keywords file is done similarly to the *Edit K-Base* option.

## 8.2.3 M-Function

*FEST* enables us to generate membership functions and to associate fuzzy variables with these membership functions. To generate a membership function, we have to provide the information requested in the following four fields:

Field 1.  *Member:* The name of the membership function.

Field 2.  *Lower:* The lower bound of the domain $X$ of the fuzzy variable.

Field 3.  *Upper:* The upper bound of the domain $X$ of the fuzzy variable.

Field 4.  *Function:* The mathematical description of the membership function in the form of $Y := f(X)$.

Assume for example, that we want to generate the fuzzy set *high_pressure* whose domain is [*0, 100*]. We enter in Field 1 the membership function's name *high_pressure*, and the domain's lower and upper bounds, *0* and *100*, in Fields 2 and 3, respectively. As far as the mathematical description of the membership function is concerned, we can specify our own function or we can use the membership functions described in Chapter 3.

We can specify our own function by entering $Y := X/100$ in Field 4, or we can generate the *S-function* of Equation (3.1), $Y := SIG(X, 40, 60, 80)$, or the *π-function* of Equation (3.2), $Y := PIE(X, 40, 60)$.

Having specified the functional relationship for the membership function, *FEST* opens a window that allow us to manipulate the membership functions file, using the following function keys.

- **F2-Ins:** Using this key, we can insert (specify) a new fuzzy set with its membership function.

- **F3-Edit:** This key allows us to edit any of the four fields described above.

- **F4-Del:** We can delete any fuzzy set from the membership functions file.

- **F5-Srch:** We can search the membership functions file for a particular entry.

- **F6-Graph:** Activating this key displays the graphical representation of the membership function associated with the selected fuzzy set.

- **F7-Val:** Occasionally we may have to specify a composite membership function by concatenating some individual membership functions. For example, we can specify the fuzzy set TALL by combining the following membership functions: $Y:=0.16X$ in the range [*0, 5*], $Y:=0.2X-0.2$ in the range [*5, 6*], and $Y:=1-SIG(X, 6, 6.5, 7)$ in the range [*6, 7*].

  In cases like this, it is important to verify that we have not specified overlapping membership functions associated with the same fuzzy set. The reason for this is that, in the fuzzification process, we need to associate every $X$ in the domain of the fuzzy set with only one corresponding $Y$ (see Chapter 10).

  The function key **F7** allows us to verify whether or not we have specified overlapping membership functions associated with the same fuzzy set. If the ranges are overlapping, *FEST* would issue an error message.

- **F8-Mod:** This function key allows us to specify *local* modifiers to modify a particular membership function. Note that using local modifiers reduces in fact the number of membership functions, and therefore increases the search speed and decreases the computation time.

  For example, we can specify the fuzzy set TALL and then provide the local modifier *very* to describe the fuzzy set VERY TALL as follows:

$$\text{VERY TALL} = SQR(\text{TALL})$$

Thus, if $X$ has the membership grade $\chi$ in the fuzzy set TALL, it will have the membership grade $\chi^2$ in the fuzzy set VERY TALL.

We will expand the discussion of *local modifiers* in Chapter 10 when we describe the fuzzy inference procedure. At this point, however, note that the local modifiers must be a subset of the modifiers defined in the modifiers list of *FEST* (see Section 8.1.3).

# 9 INFERENCE ENGINE

The expert system shell generates solutions by using a strategy that searches the knowledge base and logically derives conclusions. The part of the expert system shell that manipulates the knowledge base is called the inference engine [3, 8, 28, 40]. The inference engine determines how pieces of knowledge are related among themselves and matches of the knowledge against relevant data.

The general structure of the inference engine is shown in Figure 9.1. The inference engine is logically divided into two main parts. The first part is the *blackboard* which is responsible for storing the data provided by the user and all the intermediate results from the inference procedure. The second part of the inference engine contains the *inference procedures* which perform the inference process.

The inference procedures are based on the *modus ponens* rule. That is, given a rule $A \rightarrow B$ and the clause $A$, then the conclusion is that $B$ is true. Formally, the inference procedure can be represented as:

$$A, A \rightarrow B \vdash B \tag{9.1}$$

Thus, whenever the premise of the rule is found to be true, the rule *fires* and its conclusion must also be true.

The *modus ponens* rule can also be applied to a chain of rules as shown in Equation (9.2) below. As indicated in Equation (9.2) by the statement $x_1 \rightarrow x_n$ under the solid line, given that $x_1$ is true, then based on the *transitivity* property, we can infer that $x_n$ is also true.

$$x_1 \;\rightarrow\; x_2$$
$$x_2 \;\rightarrow\; x_3$$
$$\cdot$$
$$\cdot$$
$$\cdot$$
$$x_{n-2} \rightarrow\; x_{n-1}$$
$$x_{n-1} \rightarrow\; x_n$$

$$\rule{4cm}{0.4pt}$$

$$x_1 \;\rightarrow\; x_n \tag{9.2}$$

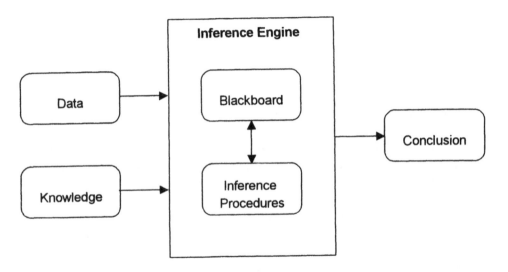

**Figure 9.1** General structure of the inference engine

In this chapter, we describe three inferencing methods: backward chaining, forward chaining, and direct chaining. The *backward chaining* inference procedure uses the tree structure for knowledge representation. It assumes a *goal* $x_j$ and then backtracks the decision tree to $x_i$ to find if $x_1$ is true. If $x_i$ is found to be true then the goal $x_j$ is said to be satisfied. This process continues recursively until the goal is satisfied.

The *forward chaining* inference procedure also uses the tree structure for knowledge representation. Here, however, $x_1$ is assumed to be true, and the inference procedure creates a path down the decision tree to establish that $x_n$ is also true.

The *direct chaining* inference procedure differs from the first two methods in that it uses the bit matrix or the relational list (R-list) to infer $x_n$ from *any* $x_i$. Thus, the direct chaining inference process is not assumed to start at the root of the decision tree nor at its terminal node.

## 9.1 Backward Chaining

Backward chaining is an inferencing method in which the inference process starts at the goal and works itself upwards [36, 56, 58]. In other words, we must first establish a goal and then find evidence to validate it (show that the goal is true). In order to validate the goal, we must show that its premise is true.

Thus, backward chaining suggests a process of recursive deductions in which we identify a goal, define the steps necessary to validate the goal (by creating a path to the top of the decision tree), and then validate each step along the path until we reach the goal.

To illustrate the backward chaining inference procedure, consider the sample knowledge base shown in Table 9.1. Careful observation of this knowledge base reveals that it contains two concluding rules, R9 and R10. Note, however, that recognizing this fact is by no means trivial.

**Table 9.1** Sample knowledge base

| | |
|---|---|
| R1 | *If A AND B, Then C* |
| R2 | *If Q, Then X* |
| R3 | *If M, Then Y* |
| R4 | *If W AND X, Then G AND Z* |
| R5 | *If D OR Z, Then E* |
| R6 | *If C AND E, Then F* |
| R7 | *If X, Then A* |
| R8 | *If Y, Then B* |
| R9 | *If F, Then S* |
| R10 | *If G, Then R* |

Hence, we want to find evidence to support the validity of rules R9 and R10. In other words, we want to verify either the conclusion of rule R9 or the conclusion of rule R10. But remember, the key phrase *backward chaining* implies that in order to verify the conclusion of some rule, we must verify its premise.

Going backwards, the construction of the backward chaining tree consists of several steps.

*Step 1*:   Rule R9 implies that we have to verify *F* in order to verify *S*. Similarly, rule R10 implies that we have to verify *G* in order to verify *R*. Since we are going backwards, these rules give rise to the tree structure shown in Figure 9.2 which depicts the first step in the construction of the backward chaining tree.,

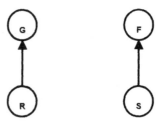

**Figure 9.2**  Step 1

*Step 2*:   The second step in the deduction process involves verifying either *F* or *G*, and it proceeds as follows.

- To verify *F*, we have to verify both *C* and *E* (rule R6).
- To verify *G*, we have to verify both *W* and *X* (rule R4).

This process is shown by the tree depicted in Figure 9.3.

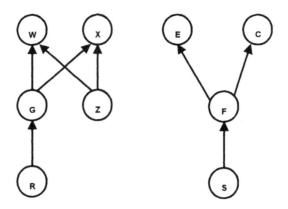

**Figure 9.3**  Step 2

*Step 3*:   We now have to verify both *C* and *E* as well as both *X* and *W*.

- To verify $C$, we have to verify both $A$ and $B$ (rule R1).
- To verify E, we have to verify either D or Z (rule R5).
- To verify $X$, we have to verify $Q$ (rule R2).
- To verify $W$, we have to *query the user* because $W$ is a starting node which is not linked-to by any other node.

The third step produces the tree shown in Figure 9.4.

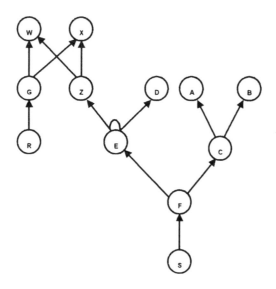

**Figure 9.4**  Step 3

*Step 4*:  This step is depicted in Figure 9.5 which shows the following.
- To verify $A$, we have to verify $X$ (rule R7).
- To verify $B$, we have to verify $Y$ (rule R8).

*Step 5*:  Verify $D$ and $Z$ (see *Step 3*).
- To verify $D$, we have to query the user because $D$ is a starting node.
- To verify $Z$, we have to verify both $W$ and $X$ (rule R4).

*Step 6*:  Verify $X$ (see *Steps 3, 4*, and *5*) and $Y$ (see *Step 4*).
- To verify $X$, we have to verify $Q$. Because $Q$ is a starting node, we verify it by querying the user.
- To verify $Y$, we have to verify $M$ (rule R3).

*Step 7*:  Verify $W$ (see *Step 5*) and $M$ (see *Step 6*).

- To verify *W*, we have to query the user because *W* is a starting node (see also *Step 3*).

- To verify *M*, we have to query the user because *M* is a starting node.

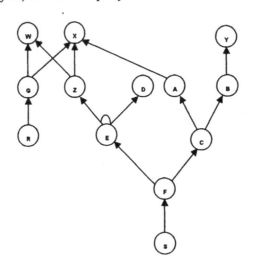

**Figure 9.5** Step 4

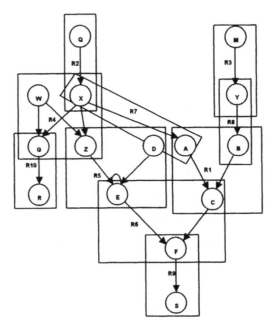

**Figure 9.6** Final tree representation of the knowledge base of Table 9.1

Lumping together the seven steps of the deduction process, Figure 9.6 above shows the final backward chaining tree representation of the knowledge base of Table 9.1. Note that, for convenience, we have "boxed-in" the rules as well as added the rule numbers to enable cross-referencing with Table 9.1.

Let us consider now the process of performing the inference with respect to the goal $S$. Assume that $Q$, $W$, and $M$ are provided by the user and are assumed to be true. Since all the data and the intermediate results are stored on the blackboard, the blackboard contains the following data:

$$blackboard = \{Q, W, M\}$$

Then, based on Figure 9.6, we have to follow the backtracking steps that are summarized in Table 9.2.

**Table 9.2** Backtracking steps for verifying the goal $S$

| |
|---|
| (1)　$S \leftarrow F$ |
| (2)　$F \leftarrow E \cap C$ |
| (3)　$E \leftarrow Z \cup D$ |
| (4)　$Z \leftarrow W \cap X$ |
| (5)　$W \leftarrow$ *query the user or search the blackboard* |
| (6)　$X \leftarrow Q$ |
| (7)　$Q \leftarrow$ *query the user or search the blackboard* |
| (8)　$D \leftarrow$ *query the user or search the blackboard* |
| (9)　$C \leftarrow A \cap B$ |
| (10)　$A \leftarrow X$ |
| (11)　$X \leftarrow Q$ |
| (12)　$Q \leftarrow$ *query the user or search the blackboard* |
| (13)　$B \leftarrow Y$ |
| (14)　$Y \leftarrow M$ |
| (15)　$M \leftarrow$ *query the user or search the blackboard* |

To show that $S$ is true, we have to show that $F$ is true {(1) in Table 9.2}. Since we have no information about $F$, we backtrack to (2) in Table 9.2. To prove that $F$ is true, we have to show that both $E$ and $C$ are true. Again, since we have no information about either $E$ or $C$, we have to backtrack (3) in Table 9.2. To prove $E$, we have to show that either $Z$ or $D$ are true.

To show $Z$, we have to prove that both $W$ and $X$ are true {(4) in Table 9.2}. To show $W$, we query the user or search the blackboard. Since $W$ is on the blackboard, we mark it true and attempt to show that $X$ is true. To show that $X$ is true, we have to show that $Q$ is true. Since $Q$ is on the blackboard, we *fire* rule R2 and place the conclusion $X$ on the blackboard, namely:

$$blackboard = \{X, Q, W, M\}$$

Now that both $W$ and $X$ are true {(5) and (6) in Table 9.2, we *fire* rule R4 and place its conclusion on the blackboard:

$$blackboard = \{G, Z, X, Q, W, M\}$$

Since $Z$ is also true, we *fire* rule R5 and conclude that $E$ is true {(3) in Table 9.2}, thus placing $E$ on the blackboard:

$$blackboard = \{E, G, Z, X, Q, W, M\}$$

To prove that $F$ is true, we have to prove that both $E$ and $C$ are true. Since we have proved only that $E$ is true and we have no information about $C$, we cannot say anything about $S$ {(1) in Table 9.2}and, therefore, we must backtrack to (9) in Table 9.2. In other words, to prove $C$, we have to prove that both $A$ and $B$ are true. Because neither $A$ nor $B$ are on the blackboard, we have to go in Table 9.2 to (10) (to prove $A$) and to (13) (to prove $B$).

To prove $A$, we have to prove $X$. But, since $X$ is on the blackboard, we *fire* rule R7 and place $A$ on the blackboard:

$$blackboard = \{A, E, G, Z, X, Q, W, M\}$$

To prove $B$, we have to show that $Y$ is true {(13) in Table 9.2}. Since $Y$ is not on the blackboard, we go to (14) in Table 9.2 where, to show that $Y$ is true, we have to show that $M$ is true. Since $M$ is on the blackboard {(15) in Table 9.2}, we *fire* rule R3 and place $Y$ on the blackboard. Now that $Y$ has been found to be true, we conclude that $B$ is also true and we can *fire* rule R8 and place $B$ on the blackboard.

$$blackboard = \{B, Y, A, E, G, Z, X, Q, W, M\}$$

Now that both $A$ and $B$ are true, we can *fire* rule R1, place $C$ on the blackboard,

$$blackboard = \{C, B, Y, A, E, G, Z, X, Q, W, M\}$$

and turn to showing that $F$ is true. To do that, we have to show that both $E$ and $C$ are true. However, since both on the blackboard, we *fire* rule R6 and place $F$ on the blackboard {(2) in Table 9.2}:

$$blackboard = \{F, C, B, Y, A, E, G, Z, X, Q, W, M\}$$

Finally, since $F$ is true, $S$ is also true {(1) in Table 9.2} and we can *fire* rule R9.

Inferencing with backward chaining is usually used in expert systems when the goal is known and the expert system's role is to find evidence to support the goal. Examples of expert systems that utilize the backward chaining inference are *MYCIN* [88], *PROSPECTOR* [18,19], and *Prolog* [93]. However, when the goal is unknown, we implement instead the forward or direct chaining methods that are considered in the following sections.

## 9.2  Forward Chaining

Inferencing via forward chaining is employed when the goal is not specified. The underlying concept of forward chaining entails the verification of the premise in order to verify that the conclusion is true. In other words, we start the inferencing procedure from the top of the decision tree and work our way to the goal [99, 101]. As we create a path in the decision tree (by firing rules), we add the intermediate conclusions to the blackboard until we reach the goal at the bottom of the decision tree.

The forward chaining inference procedure is characterized by the following.

1.    The search is a *depth-first search* [58] which guarantees that, if there is a solution, that solution will be found. That is, forward chaining is designed to find *one* solution.

2.    The inference procedure employs the blackboard as a data structure that contains the given data (if there are any) and the intermediate results.

In general, forward chaining can be classified into types of inference procedures: (i) *autonomous forward chaining*, and (ii) *interactive forward chaining*. We describe the two methods in the following sections.

### 9.2.1  Autonomous Forward Chaining

In the autonomous forward chaining inference process, the expert system is provided with the initial data and the knowledge base. The task of the inference procedure is to generate the proper decision tree based on the data and the knowledge base, match the data placed on the blackboard with the rules in the knowledge base, fire the rules, and find a terminal node that will be the conclusion.

To illustrate this type of inferencing method, consider the knowledge base of Table 9.1 and assume that, initially, the blackboard contains the following data:

$$blackboard = \{Q, W\}$$

Recall that our knowledge base has four *starting rules*, R4, R2, R5, and R3 (see Figure 9.6). For simplicity, let us begin from the left-hand side of the decision tree by trying to match the premise of rule R4 with the blackboard. We note that $W$ is on the blackboard but $X$ is not. Since $X$ can be true only if rule R2 is fired, we backtrack to rule R2 and search for its premise $Q$ on the blackboard.

Having found $Q$ on the blackboard, we *fire* rule R2 and place its conclusion on the blackboard, namely:

$$blackboard = \{X, Q, W\}$$

Now, since both $W$ and $X$ are on the blackboard, rule R4 can be *fired* and its conclusions placed on the blackboard:

$$blackboard = \{G, Z, X, Q, W\}$$

Since forward chaining is characterized by *depth-first search*, we can now *fire* rule R10 because $G$ is on the blackboard, and place its conclusion $R$ on the blackboard:

$$R \leftarrow Q, W$$

Note that, since $R$ is a terminal node, we terminate the procedure with this result.

In some expert system applications, it is important to find all possible conclusions, i.e. fire as many rules as possible. To follow this venue in our example, we have to backtrack to rule R4 and try to *fire* rule R9. In order to fire rule R9, we must first fire rule R5; however, because $Z$ is on the blackboard, rule R5 can be *fired* and its placed conclusion on the blackboard:

$$blackboard = \{E, R, G, Z, X, Q, W\}$$

For $S$, the conclusion of rule R9, to be true, the premise ($C$ and $E$) of rule R6 has to be true. We note that $E$ is on the blackboard, but $C$ is not, and therefore we halt the construction of the inference chain and backtrack to rule R1 where we see that, for $C$ to be true, both $A$ and $B$ have to be true. Because $A$ is not on the blackboard, we must backtrack to rule R7 which can be *fired* since its premise $X$ is on the blackboard. Placing the conclusion of rule R7 on the blackboard, we get:

$$blackboard = \{A, E, R, G, Z, X, Q, W\}$$

For $B$ to be true, $Y$ has to be true and to show that $Y$ is true, we have to show that $M$ is true. However, $M$ is a *starting node* and it is not on the blackboard. Consequently, we cannot *fire* rule R9 and are left with the tree shown in Figure 9.7, which is the tree of Figure 9.6 after pruning all the rules leading from node $M$.

## 9.2.2  Interactive Forward Chaining

The interactive forward chaining inference procedure assumes that a tree structure is available to the expert system. The inference engine uses the *depth-first search* to try and reach a *terminal node* by visiting each node along the path and asking the user for the truth value of a particular proposition. If the user responds positively, the inference proceeds down the tree, but if the user responds negatively, the inference engine prunes that part of the tree and attempts to find a different path. The blackboard is initially empty, and it is filled up as the rules are fired.

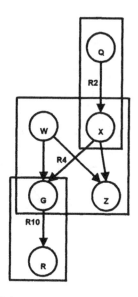

**Figure 9.7** A decision tree after pruning the node leaving $M$

To illustrate this procedure, let us reconsider the tree shown in Figure 9.6 in which there are four *starting nodes*, $W$, $Q$, $D$, and $M$. For consistency, we assume again that the inference process begins with the left-most starting node, and that the user is asked:

*Is W true?*

Suppose that the user responds negatively. Because rule R4 will never fire, it can be deleted from the tree. Furthermore, we can also delete rule R10 since its firing is dependent solely on firing rule R4. Consequently, the inference engine prunes the subtree associated with $W$, leaving us with the resulting tree shown in Figure 9.8.

Having pruned rules R4 and R10, the inference engine positions the pointer at the next starting node, which is $Q$ in our case, and prompts the user with the question:

*Is Q true?*

Assume that, now, the user responds positively to the query so that rule R2 fires and the conclusion $X$ is placed on the blackboard:

*blackboard* = $\{X\}$

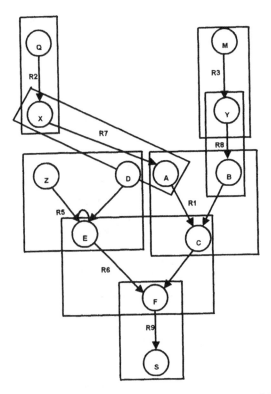

**Figure 9.8** Pruning the subtree with rules R4 and R10

Since we are using a *depth-first search*, the next step in the inference process is to move down the tree until we get stuck. In our example, our first attempt would be $A$ and since $X$ is on the blackboard, we can *fire* rule R7 and place $A$ on the blackboard, namely:

$$blackboard = \{X, A\}$$

However, at this point we cannot move down the tree any further, so we delete rules R2 and R7 from the tree. Note that we cannot prune rule R1 at this point since its firing depends on firing rule R8 whom we have not visited yet. The tree resulting from pruning rules R2 and R7 is shown in Figure 9.9.

Next, the inference engine chooses $Z$ to be the starting node (since we pruned the tree, $Z$ is now a starting node), and prompts the user with the query:

*Is Z true?*

If the user responds negatively, $Z$ is pruned from the tree and the inference engine moves to $D$, which is the next starting node, and asks the user:

*Is D true?*

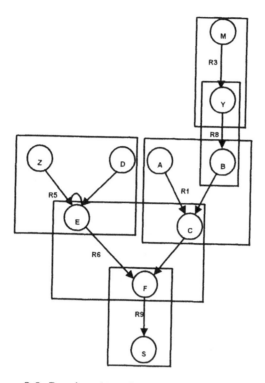

**Figure 9.9** Pruning the subtree with rules R2 and R7

Now the user responds positively so that rule R5 can be *fired* and its conclusion *E* placed on the blackboard:

$$blackboard = \{X, A, E\}$$

However, attempting to reach *F* from *E* fails since the firing of rule R6 (with the conclusion *F*) depends on *C* being true. Hence, we prune the tree of Figure 9.9, resulting in the tree shown in Figure 9.10, and look for another starting node.

The only path that remains is the one starting with *M* so the inference engine asks the user:

*Is M true?*

If the response is affirmative, rule R3 is *fired* and its conclusion *Y* is placed on the blackboard:

$$blackboard = \{X, A, E, Y\}$$

As a result (because *Y* is on the blackboard), the inference engine *fires* rule R8 and places its conclusion on the blackboard:

$$blackboard = \{X, A, E, Y, B\}$$

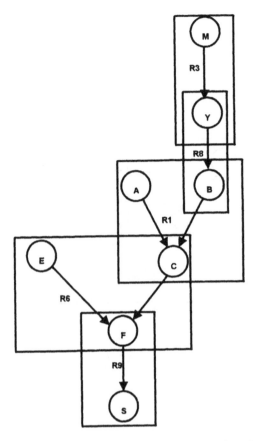

**Figure 9.10** Pruning a subtree with rule R5

With both *A* and *B* on the blackboard, rule R1 is *fired*, resulting in:

$$blackboard = \{X, A, E, Y, B, C\}$$

and since both *E* and *C* are now on the blackboard, rule R6 is *fired* with the blackboard showing:

$$blackboard = \{X, A, E, Y, B, C, F\}$$

Consequently, the inference engine *fires* rule *R9*.

The foregoing illustration of forward chaining shows that it is conceptually very simple and straightforward; however, implementing it (namely, moving up and down the tree) is far from being a trivial procedure. In contrast, the direct chaining inference process, which we use in *FEST* and discuss in the next section, was developed to simplify the inference process.

## 9.3 Direct Chaining

Direct chaining, which is the inference method used by our expert system shell *FEST*, utilizes the relational list (R-list) and other data structures to perform the inference. The term *direct* indicates that as the inference process is executing, it creates the proper chain of reasoning.

Direct chaining is designed to overcome some of the problems associated with the forward and backward chaining methods.

1. The inference process can start anywhere.

2. It is designed to find as many conclusions as possible (but can stop after the first one is found).

3. Direct chaining is very simple to implement.

4. Inferencing with direct chaining is fast.

To illustrate the direct chaining method, consider again the knowledge base in Table 9.1 and observe that we can detect the following links which lead to the relational list (R-list) shown in Table 9.3.

- *The conclusion of rule R1 is part of the premise of rule R6*
- *The conclusion of rule R2 is part of the premise of rule R4*
- *The conclusion of rule R2 is part of the premise of rule R7*
- *The conclusion of rule R3 is part of the premise of rule R8*
- *The conclusion of rule R4 is part of the premise of rule R10*
- *The conclusion of rule R4 is part of the premise of rule R5*
- *The conclusion of rule R5 is part of the premise of rule R6*
- *The conclusion of rule R6 is part of the premise of rule R9*
- *The conclusion of rule R7 is part of the premise of rule R1*
- *The conclusion of rule R8 is part of the premise of rule R1*

In addition to the relational list, we have to define the following two data structures.

1. *List of fired rules (LFR)*. Linked list containing the identifiers of *all* the rules that have been fired.

2. *List of fired concluding rules (LFC)*. Linked list containing the identifiers of the *concluding rules* that have been fired.

There are two versions of the direct chaining inference procedure: (i) *simple direct chaining* where the relational list is used to indicate whether a given rule is a concluding rule; and (ii) *fast direct chaining* where the relational list dictates the direction of the inference process.

**Table 9.3** R-list for the knowledge base of Table 9.1

| Rule # | Clause # | Rule # | Clause # | MF | MG |
|--------|----------|--------|----------|-----|-----|
| 1 | 1 | 6 | 1 | 1 | −2 |
| 2 | 1 | 4 | 2 | 1 | −2 |
| 2 | 1 | 7 | 1 | 1 | −2 |
| 3 | 1 | 8 | 1 | 1 | −2 |
| 4 | 1 | 10 | 1 | 1 | −2 |
| 4 | 2 | 5 | 1 | 1 | −2 |
| 5 | 1 | 6 | 2 | 1 | −2 |
| 6 | 1 | 9 | 1 | 1 | −2 |
| 7 | 1 | 1 | 1 | 1 | −2 |
| 8 | 1 | 1 | 2 | 1 | −2 |

*Notes:* The parameters *MF* and *MG* are defined in Equations (7.26)
and (7.25), respectively.

### 9.3.1 Simple Direct Chaining

Using the R-list and the two linked lists, *LFR* and *LFC*, we can construct a general procedure for the simple direct chaining inference process, as shown in Algorithm 9.1. The procedure begins by initializing the Boolean variable *DONE* to *FALSE* (*line 01*) and proceeds to execute the main loop of the inference procedure by repeating it for as long as there are rules that can be fired.

The body of the loop is from *line 03* to *line 15*. In *line 03*, the Boolean variable *DONE* is set to *TRUE* to indicate that, by default, we may have finished the inference process. Then, we initiate a loop that processes every rule from *1* to *N* (where *N* is the number of rules in the knowledge base). In *line 05*, we check if rule *I* was not fired in order to avoid repeated processing of rules that have already been fired. Thus, if a rule is not in the *LFR*, we get its premise and match it against the blackboard (*lines 06* and *07*). If we find a match, we fire the rule (*line 08*) and perform the following.

1.  Place the conclusion of the rule that has been fired on the blackboard (*lines 09* and *10*).

2.  Add the rule number to the *LFR* (*line 11*).

3.  If *I* is a concluding rule, then place its number in the *LFC* (*line 12*).

4.  Set the Boolean variable *DONE* to *FALSE*.

```
Line 01.  DONE := FALSE;
Line 02.  WHILE NOT DONE DO BEGIN
Line 03.     DONE := TRUE;
Line 04.     FOR I := 1 TO N DO
Line 05.     IF NOT_IN_LFR(I) THEN BEGIN
Line 06.          GET_PREMISE(ST,I);
Line 07.          COMPARE(ST,BB,MATCH);
Line 08.          IF MATCH = 1 THEN BEGIN
Line 09.               GET_CONCLUSION(CONC,I);
Line 10.               PLACE_CONCLUSION(CONC,BB);
Line 11.               ADD_TO_LFR(I);
Line 12.               IF I IS CONCLUDING RULE THEN ADD_TO_LFC(I);
Line 13.               DONE := FALSE;
Line 14.          END;     {IF}
Line 15.     END;     {IF}
Line 16. END;     {WHILE}
```

**Algorithm 9.1** Procedure for simple direct chaining

To illustrate the *simple direct chaining* inference process, refer to the knowledge base of Table 9.1, whose associated relational list is given in Table 9.3, and assume that the initial data $\{X, Y, D\}$ have been placed on the blackboard. We begin the inference procedure by setting the Boolean variable *DONE* to *FALSE* and letting $N = 10$ (since we have *10* rules in the knowledge base of Table 9.1). Then, the inference process proceeds in cycles as follows.

**Cycle 1** Check if the condition for the loop is true. Since *DONE := FALSE*, enter the loop and perform the following steps.

*Step 1.1:* Set *DONE* to *TRUE*. This will indicate that, by default, we assume that there are no more rules to fire.

*Step 1.2:* Execute the *FOR* loop:

1. Get the premise of rule R1.

2. Compare the premise $A$ and $B$ of rule R1 with the blackboard - neither $A$ nor $B$ are on the blackboard, hence, set the match to *0*.

3. Get the premise of rule R2.

4. Compare the premise $Q$ of rule R2 with the blackboard - $Q$ is not on the blackboard, hence, set the match to $0$.

5. Get the premise of rule R3.

6. Compare the premise $M$ of rule R3 with the blackboard - $M$ is not on the blackboard, hence, set the match to $0$.

7. Get the premise of rule R4.

8. Compare the premise of rule R4 with the blackboard - rule R4 cannot fire since only $X$ is on the blackboard, hence, set the match to $0$.

9. Get the premise of rule R5.

10. Compare the premise $D$ of rule R5 with the blackboard - $D$ is on the blackboard, hence, fire rule R5 and:

   - add the conclusion of rule R5 to the blackboard:

     $$blackboard = \{E, X, Y, D\}$$

   - add the rule number to the *LFR*:

     $$LFR = \{5\}$$

   - check if rule R5 is a concluding rule. Since the index of its conclusion $(5, 1)$ is in the R-list, do not add the rule's number to the *LFC*.

   - set *DONE* to *FALSE*.

11. Get the premise of rule R6.

12. Compare the premise $C$ of rule R6 with the blackboard - rule R6 cannot fire because $C$ is not on the blackboard, hence, set the match to $0$.

13. Get the premise of rule R7.

14. Compare the premise $X$ of rule R7 with the blackboard - $X$ is on the blackboard, hence, fire rule R7 and:

   - add the conclusion of rule R7 to the blackboard:

     $$blackboard = \{A, E, X, Y, D\}$$

   - add the rule number to the *LFR*:

     $$LFR = \{7, 5\}$$

   - check if rule R7 is a concluding rule. Since the index of its conclusion $(7, 1)$ is in the R-list, do not add the rule's number to the *LFC*.

   - set *DONE* to *FALSE*.

15. Get the premise of rule R8.

16. Compare the premise *Y* of rule R8 with the blackboard - *Y* is on the blackboard, hence, fire rule R8 and:

    - add the conclusion of rule R8 to the blackboard:

      $$blackboard = \{B, A, E, X, Y, D\}$$

    - add the rule number to the *LFR*:

      $$LFR = \{8, 7, 5\}$$

    - check if rule R8 is a concluding rule. Since the index of its conclusion (*8, 1*) is in the R-list, do not add the rule's number to the *LFC*.

    - set *DONE* to *FALSE*.

17. Get the premise of rule R9.

18. Compare the premise *Y* of rule R9 with the blackboard - *F* is not on the blackboard, hence, set the match to *0*.

19. Get the premise of rule R10.

20. Compare the premise *G* of rule R10 with the blackboard - *G* is not on the blackboard, hence, set match to *0*.

In the first cycle, we have fired three rules (R5, R7, and R8) and set *DONE* to *FALSE*. This means that we have to perform another cycle.

**Cycle 2** Since *DONE* := set to true, execute the *WHILE* loop.

*Step 2.1:* Set *DONE* to *TRUE*.

*Step 2.2:* Execute the *FOR* loop.

1. Get the premise of rule R1.

2. Compare the premise *A* and *B* of rule R1 with the blackboard - both *A* and *B* are now on the blackboard, hence, fire rule R1 and:

    - add the conclusion of rule R1 to the blackboard:

      $$blackboard = \{C, B, A, E, X, Y, D\}$$

    - add the rule number to the *LFR*:

      $$LFR = \{1, 8, 7, 5\}$$

    - check if rule R1 is a concluding rule. Since the index of its conclusion (*1, 1*) is in the R-list, do not add the rule's number to the *LFC*.

    - set *DONE* to *FALSE*.

3. Get the premise of rule R2.

4. Compare the premise $Q$ of rule R2 with the blackboard - $Q$ is not on the blackboard, hence, set the match to $0$.

5. Get the premise of rule R3.

6. Compare the premise $M$ of rule R3 with the blackboard - $M$ is not on the blackboard, hence, set the match to $0$.

7. Get the premise of rule R4.

8. Compare the premise $W$ of rule R4 with the blackboard - $W$ is not on the blackboard, hence, set the match to $0$.

9. Get the premise of rule R6. (Note that we skip rule R5 since it is on the blackboard.)

10. Compare the premise $C$ and $E$ of rule R6 with the blackboard - both $C$ and $E$ are on the blackboard, hence, fire rule R6 and:

   - add the conclusion of rule R6 to the blackboard:

     $$blackboard = \{F, C, B, A, E, X, Y, D\}$$

   - add the rule number to the *LFR*:

     $$LFR = \{6, 1, 8, 7, 5\}$$

   - check if rule R1 is a concluding rule. Since the index of its conclusion $(1, 1)$ is in the R-list, do not add the rule's number to the *LFC*.

   - set *DONE* to *FALSE*.

11. Get the premise of rule R9.

12. Compare the premise $F$ of rule R9 with the blackboard - $F$ is on the blackboard, hence, fire rule R9 and:

   - add the conclusion of rule R9 to the blackboard:

     $$blackboard = \{S, F, C, B, A, E, X, Y, D\}$$

   - add the rule number to the *LFR*:

     $$LFR = \{9, 6, 1, 8, 7, 5\}$$

   - check if rule R1 is a concluding rule. Since the index of its conclusion $(1, 1)$ is *not* in the R-list, add the rule's number to the *LFC*:

     $$LFC = \{9\}$$

   - Set *DONE* to *FALSE*.

13. Get the premise of rule R10.

14. Compare the premise $G$ of rule R10 with the blackboard - $G$ is not on the blackboard, hence, set the match to $0$.

The second cycle resulted in firing three more rules (R1, R6, and R9 which is a concluding rule), and with the Boolean variable *DONE* set to *FALSE*. Therefore, we have to perform another cycle of inferencing.

**Cycle 3** Since *DONE := FALSE*, execute the *WHILE* loop.

*Step 3.1:* Set *DONE* to *TRUE*.

*Step 3.2:* Execute the *FOR* loop.

1.  Get the premise of rule R2.
2.  Compare the premise $Q$ of rule R2 with the blackboard - $Q$ is not on the blackboard, hence, set the match to *0*.
3.  Get the premise of rule R3.
4.  Compare the premise $M$ of rule R2 with the blackboard - $M$ is not on the blackboard, hence, set the match to *0*.
5.  Get the premise of rule R4.
6.  Compare the premise $W$ of rule R4 with the blackboard - $W$ is not on the blackboard, hence, set the match to *0*.
7.  Get the premise of rule R10.
8.  Compare the premise $G$ of rule R10 with the blackboard - $G$ is not on the blackboard, hence, set the match to *0*.

At this point, no more rules have been fired and the Boolean variable *DONE:=TRUE*, indicating the termination of the inference process. Consequently, we conclude that:

*Given that X, Y and D are true, S is true*


### 9.3.2  Fast Direct Chaining

The fast direct chaining inference process takes advantage of the relational list and the *depth-first search* to find as many conclusions as possible. The inference process can start anywhere in the reasoning chain and follows the algorithm depicted in Algorithm 9.2.

The direct chaining inference procedure requires one pass through the knowledge base. *Lines 10* to *12* in Algorithm 9.2 indicate that if a link exists, it should be established and the inference procedure should be performed recursively.

To illustrate the *fast direct chaining* inference process, consider the knowledge base of Table 9.1, whose associated relational list is given in Table 9.2, and assume that the initial data $\{X, Y, D\}$ has been placed on the blackboard. Let $N = 10$ (since we have *10* rules in the knowledge base of Table 9.1) and proceed as follows.

*Step 1:*   Get the premise of rule R1.

*Step 2:*    Compare the premise $A$ and $B$ of rule R1 with the blackboard - $A$ and $B$ are not on the blackboard, hence, set the match to $0$.

*Step 3:*    Get the premise of rule R2.

---

*Line 01.* FOR I := 1 TO N DO

*Line 02.* IF NOT_IN_LFR(I) THEN BEGIN

*Line 03.*     GET_PREMISE(ST,I);

*Line 04.*     COMPARE(ST,BB,MATCH);

*Line 05.*     IF MATCH = 1 THEN BEGIN

*Line 06.*         GET_CONCLUSION(CONC,I);

*Line 07.*         PLACE_CONCLUSION(CONC,BB);

*Line 08.*         ADD_TO_LFR(I);

*Line 09.*         IF I IS CONCLUDING RULE THEN ADD_TO_LFC(I)

*Line 10.*         ELSE {THERE IS A LINKAGE} THEN BEGIN

*Line 11.*             OBTAIN THE NEW RULE NUMBER J;

*Line 12.*             SET (TEMPORARILY) I:=J;

*Line 13.*             IF J IS NOT IN LFR THEN GO TO 03

*Line 14.*         END;    {IF}

*Line 15.*     END;    {IF}

*Line 16.* END;    {IF}

---

**Algorithm 9.2** Procedure for fast direct chaining

*Step 4:*    Compare the premise $Q$ of rule R2 with the blackboard - $Q$ is not on the blackboard, hence, set the match to $0$.

*Step 5:*    Get the premise of rule R3.

*Step 6:*    Compare the premise $M$ of rule R3 with the blackboard - $M$ is not on the blackboard, hence, set the match to $0$.

*Step 7:*    Get the premise of rule R4.

*Step 8:*    Compare the premise $W$ and $X$ of rule R4 with the blackboard - $W$ is not on the blackboard, hence, set the match to $0$.

*Step 9:*    Get the premise of rule R5.

*Step 10:*   Compare the premise $D$ of rule R5 with the blackboard - $D$ is on the blackboard, hence, fire rule R5 and:

1. place the conclusion $E$ of rule R5 on the blackboard:

$$blackboard = \{E, X, Y, D\}$$

2. add rule R5 to the *LFR*:

$$LFR = \{5\}$$

4. check if rule R5 is a concluding rule - rule R5 is not a concluding rule.

5. find linkage - according to the R-list, rule R5 is linked to rule R6, hence, set $I = 6$ and recursively go to *line 03*:

- get the premise of rule R6

- compare the premise $C$ of rule R6 with the blackboard - $C$ is not on the blackboard, hence, set the match to *0*. Since this was a recursive call from *Step 10.4*, backtrack to *Step 10.4* and continue.

*Step 11:* Get the premise of rule R6.

*Step 12:* Compare the premise $C$ of rule R6 with the blackboard - $C$ is not on the blackboard, hence, set the match to *0*.

*Step 13:* Get the premise of rule R7.

*Step 14:* Compare the premise $X$ of rule R7 with the blackboard - $X$ is on the blackboard, hence, fire rule R7 and:

1. place the conclusion $A$ of rule R7 on the blackboard:

$$blackboard = \{A, E, X, Y, D\}$$

2. add R7 to the *LFR*:

$$LFR = \{7, 5\}$$

3. check if rule R7 is a concluding rule - rule R7 is not a concluding rule.

4. find linkage - according to the R-list, rule R7 is linked to rule R1, hence, set $I := 1$ and recursively go to *line 03*:

- get the premise of rule R1

- compare the premise $B$ of rule R1 with the blackboard - $B$ is not on the blackboard, hence, set the match to *0* and return to *Step 14.4*.

*Step 15:* Get the premise of rule R8.

*Step 16:* Compare the premise $Y$ of rule R8 with the blackboard - $Y$ is on the blackboard, hence, fire rule R8 and:

1. place the conclusion $B$ of rule R8 on the blackboard:

$$blackboard = \{B, A, E, X, Y, D\}$$

2. add R8 to the *LFR*:

$$LFR = \{8, 7, 5\}$$

3.  check if rule R8 is a concluding rule - rule R8 is not a concluding rule.

4.  find linkage - according to the R-list, rule R8 is linked to rule R1, hence, set $I := 1$, and recursively go to *line 03*:

-   get the premise of rule R1

-   compare the premise $A$ and $B$ of rule R1 with the blackboard - both $A$ and $B$ are on the blackboard, hence, fire rule R1 and:

    -   place the conclusion $C$ of rule R1 on the blackboard:

        $$blackboard = \{C, B, A, E, X, Y, D\}$$

    -   add rule R1 to the *LFR*:

        $$LFR = \{1, 8, 7, 5\}$$

-   check if rule R1 is a concluding rule - rule R1 is not a concluding rule

-   find linkage - according to the R-list, rule R1 is linked to rule R6, hence, set $I := 6$ and recursively go to *line 03*:

    -   get the premise of rule R6

    -   compare the premise $C$ and $E$ of rule R6 with the blackboard - both $C$ and $E$ are on the blackboard, hence, fire rule R6 and:

        -   place the conclusion $F$ of rule R6 on the blackboard:

            $$blackboard = \{F, C, B, A, E, X, Y, D\}$$

        -   add rule R6 to the *LFR*:

            $$LFR = \{6, 1, 8, 7, 5\}$$

    -   check if rule R6 is a concluding rule - rule R6 is not a concluding rule

    -   find linkage - according to the R-list, rule R6 is linked to rule R9, hence, set $I := 9$ and recursively go to *line 03*:

        -   get the premise of rule R9

        -   compare the premise $F$ of rule R9 with the blackboard - $F$ is on the blackboard, hence, fire rule R9 and:

            -   place the conclusion $S$ of rule R9 on the blackboard:

                $$blackboard = \{S, F, C, B, A, E, X, Y, D\}$$

            -   add rule R9 to the *LFR*:

                $$LFR = \{9, 6, 1, 8, 7, 5\}$$

            -   check if rule R9 is a concluding rule - rule R9 is a concluding rule. Hence, add the rule number to *LFC*:

$$LFC = \{9\}$$

*Step 17:* Get the premise of rule R10.

*Step 18:* Compare the premise $G$ of rule R10 with the blackboard - $G$ is not on the blackboard, hence, set the match to 0.

Since we have finished the main loop, we terminate the inference process and conclude that:

*Given that X, Y and D are true, S is true*

As can be seen, the *fast* direct chaining inference process is more efficient than the *simple* direct chaining inference process because it revisits only the rules that may potentially contribute to the inference process. In the example shown, Rules 2, 3, 4, and 10 have been visited only once.

The direct chaining is the simplest method of inference. It attempts to fire as many rules as possible, and the list of fired concluding rules ($LFC$) indicates if the process is successful or not. However, none of the inference procedures described in this chapter is capable of operating in fuzzy environments. In the next chapter we will explain how the fuzzy direct chaining procedure is designed to infer in fuzzy environments.

# 10 THE FUZZY INFERENCE ENGINE

The fuzzy inference process is a *breadth-first* search algorithm that is based on the direct chaining inference process described in the previous chapter and on the preprocessing stage discussed in Chapter 7.

The fuzzy inference process consists of the following components:

1. list of fired rules (LFR)

2. list of fired concluding rules (LFC)

3. relational list (R-list)

4. matching engine

5. inference engine

The inference process is invoked after data have been entered into a blackboard. The inference engine evaluates each rule in the knowledge base, and matches the premise clauses against clauses in the blackboard. If the certainty factor of the premise is greater than some threshold value, the rule is fired. Then, the relational list is searched for this rule number: if it is *not* found, the rule becomes a *concluding rule*; otherwise, the process repeats with the rule specified by the premise part of the relational list. At the end of the process, the list of conclusions is returned to the user.

The inference process, summarized in Algorithm 10.1, is divided into two stages.

1. In the first stage, we process the premise by matching the data stored in the blackboard against the clauses of the premise of a given rule.

2.   If the rule fires (the certainty of the premise is greater than a given threshold), then in the second stage, we process the conclusion by searching the R-list for possible linkages. If a linkage is found, then the inference process is invoked recursively, starting with the rule that is linked to the fired rule.

---

*FOR I = 1 TO NumberOfRules DO BEGIN*

  *IF RULE I IS NOT IN LFR THEN BEGIN*

    *PROCESS PREMISE OF RULE I.*

    *IF THRESHOLD IS EXCEEDED THEN FIRE RULE I*

      *AND PROCESS THE CONCLUSION.*

  *END*

*END*

---

**Algorithm 10.1**  The inference process

To avoid firing the same rule more than once, the algorithm includes a test that checks if the rule has already been fired. If a rule has fired (the certainty of the premise is greater than the given threshold), the rule number is added to the *list of fired rules (LFR)* (see Section 10.2.2) and this list is checked during inferencing to prevent the inference engine from firing the same rule more than once.

In the next two sections, we describe the two stages of the inference process, premise processing and conclusion processing. We then provide a comprehensive example to illustrate the overall performance of the fuzzy inference engine.

## 10.1  Premise Processing

Processing a premise consists of matching each clause in the premise against the data placed on the blackboard and, then, of evaluating the overall certainty in that premise. This is done in order to determine if a rule can be fired (recall that a rule is said to be fired if its premise certainty is greater than a given threshold). If a rule is fired, then we proceed to the next step in the inference process, namely, processing the conclusion of the rule.

The inference engine follows three steps in order to determine the overall certainty of a premise.

1.   matching the clauses against the blackboard

2.   evaluating the certainty of the premise

3.   updating the certainty of the premise with the conclusion certainty (see Chapter 6).

We describe these three steps in the following sections.

## 10.1.1 Matching Clauses

The general algorithm for matching the clauses in the premise against the blackboard is outlined in Algorithm 10.2. Note that in this procedure, the variable $I$ is the number of clauses in a particular premise.

---

*FOR I:= 1 TO NumberOfClausesInPremise DO BEGIN*

   *GET CLAUSE I;*

   *MATCH CLAUSE I AGAINST THE BLACKBOARD;*

*END;*

---

**Algorithm 10.2** Procedure for matching clauses

Each clause in the premise, or on the blackboard, can be one of the following types (see Chapter 7 for details):

1.   $R_c^M$ - Regular clause that is associated with some membership function.

2.   $R_c^{\overline{M}}$ - Regular clause that is not associated with a membership function.

3.   $M_c$ - Mathematical expression.

4.   $E_c$. - Executable clause.

In the following paragraphs we compute the *degree of similarity* (*MF*) and the *degree of membership* (*MG*) for any combination of clauses (see Section 7.3).

### *Matching $R_c^M$ with $R_c^M$*

When the two clauses are associated with membership functions, the structure of both is $X$ *is* $Y$ where $Y$ is a *word*. Let the clause $c_1$ be of the form $X$ *is* $Y$ and let the second clause $c_2$ be of the form $X^*$ *is* $Y^*$. Then, the *matching factor* between the two clauses is given by:

$$M = \begin{cases} 1 & \text{if } X = X^* \text{ and } Y = Y^* \\ 0 & \text{otherwise} \end{cases} \tag{10.1}$$

so that the degree of similarity *MF* is either *1* or *0*, and the degree of membership of one clause with respect to the other is given by:

$$MG = \begin{cases} U & \text{if } X = X^* \text{ and } Y = Y^* \\ -2 & \text{otherwise} \end{cases}$$

(10.2)

In Equation (10.2), $MG = U$ denotes that the membership grade cannot be evaluated whereas $MG = -2$ indicates that the clauses are associated with different membership functions and therefore cannot be matched.

## *Matching $R_c^M$ with $R_c^{\overline{M}}$*

Let $c_1$ be the clause associated with some membership function, $c_1 : X$ is $Y$, where $Y$ is a *word*, and let the second clause $c_2$ be of the form $X^*$ *is $Y^*$* as described in Chapter 7. Then, we have to consider the following cases.

1.  $Y^*$ *in $c_2$ is a word.* We compute the degree of similarity and the degree of membership similarly to the previous paragraph. Note that if $Y = Y^*$, then $Y^*$ has to be associated with the same membership function as $Y$.

2.  $Y^*$ *in $c_2$ is a number.* Here we can compute the grade of membership of $Y^*$ in $Y$. The matching factor is set to 1, that is:

$$MF = \begin{cases} 1 & \text{if } X = X^* \text{ and } MG = -2 \\ 0 & \text{otherwise} \end{cases}$$

(10.3)

and

$$MG = \begin{cases} \chi_Y(Y^*) & \text{if } X = X^* \\ -2 & \text{otherwise} \end{cases}$$

(10.4)

**Example 10.1:** Let $c_1$ be *pressure is high*, with the membership function *high_pressure* defined as $\pi(40, 60)$ in the domain $[0, 100]$ (see Equation (3.2)), and let $c_2$ be *pressure is 70*. Then, *MF* is set to *1* and *MG* is set to *0.88* because $\chi_{high\_pressure}(70) = 0.88$.

3.  $Y^*$ *in $c_2$ is an interval.* In this case, we compute the mid-point of the interval and then compute *MF* and *MG* following to Equations (10.3) and (10.4), respectively. Let $c_2$ be $X^*$ *is $N_1$ to $N_2$*, where $N_1$ and $N_2$ designate the interval's bounds. Then, the interval's mid-point $N$ is given by,

$$N = \frac{N_1 + N_2}{2}$$

(10.5a)

and the two parameters, $MF$ and $MG$, are computed as:

$$MF = \begin{cases} 1 & if\ X = X^* \\ 0 & otherwise \end{cases} \tag{10.5b}$$

and

$$MG = \begin{cases} \chi_Y(N) & if\ X = X^* \\ -2 & otherwise \end{cases} \tag{10.5c}$$

**Example 10.2:** Let $c_1$ be *pressure is high* and $c_2$ be *pressure is 30 to 50*. Also, let *high_pressure* be a fuzzy variable associated with the membership function $\pi(40, 60)$ in the domain $[0, 100]$ (see Equation (3.2)). The mid-point of $c_2$'s interval $[30, 50]$ is $N = \frac{1}{2}(30 + 50) = 40$, and $MF$ and $MG$ calculated according to Equations (10.3) and (10.4) are given by:

$$MF = 1$$

and

$$MG = \chi_{high\_pressure}(40) = 0.5$$

4.   $c_2$ *is in the form* $X^*$ *is MOD* $N_1$. Recalling that $MOD$ designates a modifier and $N_1$ is some number, the first step is to create the interval associated with $Y^*$ according to Table 7.2:

$$\begin{aligned} LB &= N_1 \cdot \downarrow \\ UB &= N_1 \cdot \uparrow \end{aligned} \tag{10.6}$$

Then, we use Equation (10.5a) to find the interval's mid-point $N$ and use Equations (10.5b) and (10.5c) to compute $MF$ and $MG$.

**Example 10.3:** Let $c_1$ be *pressure is high* with the same membership function as before, and let $c_2$ be *pressure is almost 40*, where *almost* is a modifier with $\downarrow = 0.95$ and $\uparrow = 1$. First, we use Equation (10.6) to evaluate the interval generated by the modifier *almost*:

$$LB = 40 \times 0.95 = 38$$
$$UB = 40 \times 1.00 = 40$$

Next, we compute the interval's mid-point according to Equation (10.5a):

$$N = \frac{1}{2}(38 + 40) = 39$$

Finally, we apply Equations (10.5b) and (10.5c) to compute $MF$ and $MG$:

$$MF = 1$$

and

$$MG = \chi_{high\_pressure}(39) = 0.45$$

5.  $c_2$ *is in the form* $X^*$ *is MOD* $N_1$ *to* $N_2$. This case is similar to the preceding case 4. We compute the interval according to Table 7.2 and then proceed according to the previous case.

6.  $c_2$ *is in the form* $X^*$ *is NOT MOD* $Y^*$. Since $Y^*$ is not a *word* (we have already explored this case), then using Table 7.3, we compute the two intervals associated with $Y^*$, denoting them [$N1$, $N2$] and [$N3$, $N4$], and set $MF = 1$ and $MG = U$ (see also Chapter 7).

So far, we have assumed that $c_1 : X$ is $Y$. However, to describe $Y$ it is possible to insert a modifier and/or *NOT* operator in the clause. It is important to note that the modifier in this case is a *local* modifier (a subset of the set of modifiers) which is associated with the particular membership function (see Chapter 8). Hence, to compute the degree of membership $MG$ we have to consider three cases in which $c_1$ is $X$ is MOD $Y$, $X$ is NOT $Y$, or $X$ is NOT MOD $Y$, whereas for all these three cases, the degree of similarity $MF = 1$.

1.  $c_1 : X$ *is MOD* $Y$, *and* $c_2$ *is in any of the forms described above.* We compute the interval's midpoint $N$ and use it to compute the grade of membership $\chi_Y(N)$. Designating by $V$ the value of the local modifier, we update the grade of membership $\chi_Y(N)$ according to the modifier as follows:

$$\chi_Y(N) = \chi_Y(N) \cdot V \qquad (10.7)$$

and use the new value of $\chi_Y(N)$ in Equation (10.5c) to compute the degree of membership $MG$.

**Example 10.4:** Let $c_1$ be *pressure is almost high*, where the value of the modifier *almost* is $V = 0.9$ and the fuzzy variable *high_pressure* is associated with the membership function $\pi(40, 60)$. Also, let $c_2$ be *the pressure is 40*.

Since $\chi_{high\_pressure}(40) = 0.5$, we use Equation (10.7) to update grade of membership, namely:

$$\chi_{high\_pressure}(almost\ 40) = 0.5 \times 0.9$$
$$= 0.45$$

Hence, $MG = 0.45$.

2.  $c_1 : X$ *is NOT* $Y$, *and* $c_2$ *is in any of the forms described above.* We compute the interval's midpoint $N$ and use it to compute the grade of membership $\chi_Y(N)$. We then apply the *NOT* operator to update the grade of membership $\chi_Y(N)$ as follows:

$$\chi_Y(N) = 1 - \chi_Y(N) \qquad (10.8)$$

and use the new value of $\chi_Y(N)$ in Equation (10.5c) to compute the degree of membership $MG$.

**Example 10.5:** Let $c_1$ be *pressure is not high* and let the fuzzy variable *high_pressure* be associated with the membership function $\pi(40, 60)$. Also, let $c_2$ be *the pressure is 50*.

Since $\chi_{high\_pressure}(50) = 0.88$, we use Equation (10.8) to update the grade of membership, namely:

$$\chi_{high\_pressure}(NOT\ 50) = 1 - 0.88$$
$$= 0.12$$

Hence, $MG = 0.12$.

3. $c_1 : X\ is\ NOT\ MOD\ Y$, *and* $c_2$ *is in any of the forms described above*. Here, we combine the previous two cases. We compute the interval's midpoint $N$ and use it to compute the grade of membership $\chi_Y(N)$. Then, we update $\chi_Y(N)$ in two steps: first, with the local modifier using Equation (10.7); second, by applying the *NOT* operator using Equation (10.8).

**Example 10.6:** Let $c_1$ be *pressure is not almost high*, and let $c_2$ be *the pressure is 50*. The fuzzy variable *high_pressure* is associated with the membership function $\pi(40, 60)$ and the *local* modifier *almost* has a value of $V = 0.9$.

Since $\chi_{high\_pressure}(50) = 0.88$, we use Equation (10.7) to update it according to the local modifier *almost*:

$$\chi_{high\_pressure}(almost\ 50) = 0.88 \times 0.9$$
$$= 0.79$$

and then further update it by applying the *NOT* operator using Equation (10.8):

$$\chi_{high\_pressure}(not\ almost\ 50) = 1 - 0.79$$
$$= 0.21$$

Hence, $MG = 0.21$.

## *Matching $R_c^M$ with $M_c$*

When we match a regular clause with a mathematical clause, we have to distinguish between two cases. Designating the regular clause $c_1$ and the mathematical clause by $c_2$, we have the following.

1.   $c_1 : X$ *is* $Y$ and $c_2 :$ [*expr$_1$* < *op* > *expr$_2$*], where *expr$_1$* and *expr$_2$* are mathematical expressions and *op* is some relation (see Section 7.3.7). In this case, we set *MF* to *0* and *MG* to *U* (see Equation (10.2)) because we cannot compare a logical expression with a regular clause.

**Example 10.7:** Let $c_1$ be *pressure is not almost high*, and let $c_2$ be *pressure < 50*. The fuzzy variable *high_pressure* is associated with the membership function $\pi(40, 60)$, and the value of the *local* modifier *almost* is $V = 0.9$. Clearly, regardless of the evaluation of $c_2$, it makes sense to compare the two.

2.   $c_1 : X$ *is* $Y$ and $c_2 :$ [$X^* := expr$], where $X^*$ is a variable and *expr* is some mathematical expression. If *expr* can be evaluated, then we can rewrite the expression as $X^*$ *is* $N$, where $N$ is the result of the evaluation, and match the two clauses as we did in the previous section.

**Example 10.8:** Let $c_1$ be *pressure is not almost high*, and let $c_2$ be [*pressure := SQR(X)/8*], with $X = 20$. The fuzzy variable *high_pressure* is associated with the membership function $\pi(40, 60)$, and the value of the *local* modifier *almost* is $V = 0.9$.

Evaluating the mathematical expression yields $N = 50$ so that it can be rewritten as *pressure is 50*. With $c_2$ evaluated, we obtain $\chi_{high\_pressure}(50) = 0.88$ and can, therefore, update it using Equations (10.7) and (10.8):

$$\chi_{high\_pressure}(almost\ 50) = 0.88 \times 0.9$$
$$= 0.79$$

and

$$\chi_{high\_pressure}(not\ almost\ 50) = 1 - 0.79$$
$$= 0.21$$

Hence, $MG = 0.21$. To establish $MF$, we note that $X = X^*$. Therefore, following Equation (10.5b), we set $MF$ to $1$.

### *Matching $R_c^M$ with $E_c$*

As explained in Section 7.3.4, we cannot match an executable clause with any other clause. Thus, if $c_1$ is a regular clause and $c_2$ is an executable clause, then

$$MF = 0 \quad if\ c_2 \in E_c \tag{10.9}$$

and the degree of membership $MG$ is set to $U$ (see Equation(10.2)).

*Matching* $R_c^{\overline{M}}$ *with* $R_c^{\overline{M}}$

When we match two regular clauses that are not associated with membership functions, the process is identical to the one described in Section 7.3.2. If $c_1 : X$ *is* $Y$ and $c_2 : X^*$ *is* $Y^*$, then $Y$ or $Y^*$ can be a *word*, a *number*, an *interval*, or a *double interval*.

**Example 10.9:** Let the premise clause $c_1$ be *pressure is not 50 to 60*, and the clause in the blackboard $c_2$ be *pressure is more_or_less 48*. Also, assume that the range of the domain is [*0, 100*] and that the modifier *more_or_less* generates $\downarrow = 0.9$ and $\uparrow = 1.1$.

The degree of membership *MG* is set to –2, and the degree of similarity *MF* is computed as follows.

1. Check if $X = X^*$. It is in this example because both are the word *pressure*.

2. Parse both clauses and assign values to the proper intervals (intervals $A$ and $B$ to the premise clause and intervals $C$ and $D$ to the clause in the blackboard):

$$A = [0, 50]$$

$$B = [60, 100]$$

$$C = [43.2, 52.8]$$

$D = $ *undefined because the blackboard clause does not contain a negation*

3. Apply Equation (7.31) to compute the *matching factor*:

$$M = \frac{I(A,C)+I(B,C)}{w(C)}$$

$$= \frac{6.8+0}{9.6}$$

$$= 0.71$$

Hence, the degree of similarity *MF = 0.71*.

*Matching* $R_c^{\overline{M}}$ *with* $M_c$

The matching process of a regular clause with a mathematical clause is the one described in Section 7.3.3. If $c_1 : X$ *is* $Y$, where $Y$ is not a fuzzy variable, then we have two cases to consider:

1. $c_2$ *is a logical expression.* We try to evaluate it regardless of the structure of $c_1$. In other words, we do not perform any matching between $c_1$ and $c_2$ and,

therefore, we set the degree of similarity *MF* to the result of the evaluation of the logical expression.

2.   $c_2$ : [$X^*$ := *expression*]. We evaluate the expression and then match the two clauses, as we did in the previous cases, to establish the degree of similarity *MF*.

In both cases, the degree of membership *MG* is set to –2.

### *Matching* $M_c$ *with* $M_c$

The clause in the blackboard can be a mathematical expression [$X$ := *expression*], and the premise clause can be a logical expression [*expression$_1$* < *op* > *expression$_2$*]. Since the logical expression is evaluated regardless of the structure of the clause in the blackboard, we set the degree of similarity *MF* to the result of the evaluation (of the logical expression) and set the degree of membership *MG* to –2.

### 10.1.2  Updating The Matching Factor

It is important to note that when the user provides data to the expert system, each proposition can be associated with some uncertainty measure (see Chapter 6). In other words, each clause in the data set is associated with some data certainty *DC*, and this data certainty is factored in the final evaluation of the matching process between any blackboard clause and a premise clause.

   Let $c_p$ and $c_{bb}$ be the premise and blackboard clauses, respectively. Then, the certainty factor which is associated with any premise clause and denoted $CF_{c_p}$ is computed as:

$$CF_{c_p} = MF(c_p, c_{bb}) \cdot DC \qquad (10.10)$$

### 10.1.3  Evaluating The Certainty Of The Premise

The process of clause matching involves matching each clause in the premise against every clause on the blackboard. When this process is completed, each clause in the premise is associated with some certainty factor.

   The general structure of a premise *P* can be represented in the following *BNF* notation:

$$P = (P) \mid P \mid P \text{ } AND \text{ } P \mid P \text{ } OR \text{ } P \mid c$$

where *c* is any clause. The computation of the certainty factor of the entire premise is based on this *BNF* notation.

Let the certainty factor of the premise be $CF_P$ and the certainty factor of any clause $i$ in the premise be $CF_{c_i}$. Then, for any two clauses $i$ and $j$ we can compute the *integrated* certainty factor in the following way.

1. For the portion of the premise that contains $c_i$ AND $c_j$, $CF_P$ is given by:

$$CF_P = min(CF_{c_i}, CF_{c_j}) \qquad (10.11)$$

2. For the portion of the premise that contains $c_i$ OR $c_j$, $CF_P$ is given by:

$$CF_P = max(CF_{c_i}, CF_{c_j}) \qquad (10.12)$$

3. In cases where the premise contains only one clause, then:

$$CF_P = CF_{c_i} \qquad (10.13)$$

The evaluation process of the premise is a recursive procedure based on the *BNF* notation described above.

When the computation of the integrated certainty factor of the premise is completed, the same process is repeated to compute the *cumulative* membership grade for the entire premise. Let $MB_P$ be the membership function of the premise, and let $MB_{c_i}$ and $MB_{c_j}$ be membership grades associated with clauses $i$ and $j$, respectively. Then, we compute the overall membership grade of the premise in the following way:

1. If one of the clauses is assigned the membership grade $U$, then for the portion of the premise that contains $c_i$ AND $c_j$, $MB_P$ is defined as:

$$MB_P = min(U, MG_{c_j}) = MG_{c_j} \qquad (10.14)$$

and

$$MB_P = min(-2, MG_{c_j}) = MG_{c_j} \qquad (10.15)$$

2. If one of the clauses is assigned the membership grade $U$, then for the portion of the premise that contains $c_i$ OR $c_j$, $MB_P$ is defined as:

$$MB_P = max(U, MG_{c_j}) = MG_{c_j} \qquad (10.16)$$

and

$$MB_P = max(-2, MG_{c_j}) = MG_{c_j} \qquad (10.17)$$

3. If the membership grades of both clauses differ from $U$, then for the portion of the premise that contains $c_i$ AND $c_j$, $MB_P$ is defined as:

$$MB_P = min(MG_{c_i}, MG_{c_j}) \qquad (10.18)$$

4. If the membership grades of both clauses differ from $U$, then for the portion of the premise that contains $c_i$ OR $c_j$, $MB_P$ is defined as:

$$MB_P = max(MG_{c_i}, MG_{c_j})$$                                (10.19)

Having evaluated the *integrated* certainty factor and the *cumulative* membership grade, every premise is now associated with some $CF_P$ and $MB_P$. These two values are carried to next step in Section 10.1.4 below which updates the overall certainty factor of the premise.

### 10.1.4 Final Adjustment Of CFp

The *conclusion certainty* (CC) (referred to as the *conclusion confidence* in Section 7.1) measures the relationship between the premise and the conclusion. In other words, given that the premise is true to a certain degree, CC measures the truth of the conclusion. The certainty in the conclusion is provided to the expert system when the user enters the rules.

Let $CF_P$ be the certainty factor of the premise and let $CC_R$ be the conclusion certainty of the rule. Then, the *adjusted* certainty of the premise is computed using the following assignment:

$$CF_P \leftarrow CF_P \cdot CC_R$$                                (10.20)

The adjusted certainty factor of the premise is compared with the threshold $T$ provided by the user (see Chapter 8) so that:

$$If\ CF_P > T,\ Then\ the\ rule\ is\ fired$$                        (10.21)

If the rule is fired, we proceed to process the conclusion.

## 10.2  Conclusion Processing

The conclusion of the rule is processed only if the *adjusted* certainty factor of the premise of the rule is greater than the user-provided threshold. This process consists of four steps, described in the following sections.

1.   Computing the certainty of the conclusion.
2.   Updating the list of fired rules (*LFR*).
3.   Updating (if necessary) the list of fired concluding rules (*LFC*).
4.   Using the relational list (*R-list*) for processing additional rules.

### 10.2.1  Computing The Certainty Of The Conclusion

Recall from Chapter 7 that the overall weight $W_{R_i}$ of rule $R_i$ is a subjective measure that accumulates some of the uncertainties associated with the given rule (see

Equation (7.1)). Furthermore, in computing the overall certainty of a given conclusion, we have to account for $CF_P$, the uncertainty computed for the premise of the rule and passed to the conclusion.

The total certainty associated with each clause in the conclusion of a given rule, denoted $CF_{C_q}$, is defined as:

$$CF_{C_q} = min(CF_P, W_{R_i})$$ (10.22)

where $CF_P$ is given by Equation (10.20).

The degree of membership $MG$ computed in the premise part affects a conclusion clause if that clause is associated with some membership function. There are three cases to consider.

1.  If the clause associated with the membership function is not a concluding clause (that is, its ID is found in the relational list (see Chapter 5)), then the membership grade of the conclusion is set to the membership grade of the premise.

2.  If the membership grade computed in the premise part of the rule is not $U$, and if the clause in the conclusion part of the rule is a concluding clause, then we compute the *inverse membership grade*, denoted $\chi^{-1}$, of the concluding clause. This process is referred to as the *defuzzification process*.

    Let $Y$ be the fuzzy set associated with the concluding clause, and let $MG$ be the degree of membership computed in the premise part of the rule. Then, for triangular or bell-shaped membership functions (see Equation (3.2)), the inverse membership grade is computed as follows:

$$\chi_Y^{-1}(n) = \frac{\chi_Y^{-1}(n_1) + \chi_Y^{-1}(n_2)}{2}$$ (10.23a)

However, for monotonic membership functions (see Equation (3.1)), the inverse membership grade is computed as follows:

$$\chi_Y^{-1} = \chi_Y^{-1}(n)$$ (10.23b)

The following example serves to illustrate the application of Equation (10.233a) as well as to explain the parameters $n_1$, $n_2$, and $n$.

**Example 10.9:** Assume that the degree of membership computed in the premise of the rule is $MG = 0.9$, and that the membership function associated with the concluding clause is $TRI(20, 50, 80)$[1] depicted in Figure 10.1. The

---

[1] The TRI function accepts three points $\alpha$, $\beta$, $\gamma$ and creates a triangle in which $\alpha$ designates the left-most point in the triangle, $\gamma$ represents the right-most point of the triangle, and $\beta$ represents the point where the membership grade is 1.

figure shows the parameters $n_1$ and $n_2$ that correspond to $MG = 0.9$ and the corresponding inverse membership grades $\chi_Y^{-1}(n_1) = 47$, $\chi_Y^{-1}(n_2) = 53$, and $\chi_Y^{-1}(n) = 50$ where $n$ refers to the midpoint of *47* and *53*.

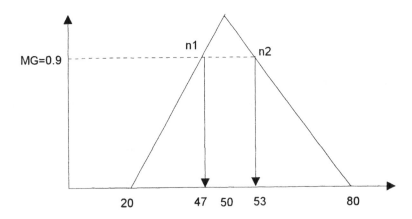

**Figure 10.1** Computing the inverse membership grade

3.    If the membership grade computed by the premise part of the rule is set to $U$, then it will not affect the clause in the conclusion part of the rule that is associated with the membership function. This is because we cannot compute the inverse membership grade $\chi^{-1}$. Hence, if the clause is a concluding clause, then nothing is done, and if the clause is not a concluding clause, then the membership grade associated with that clause is also set to $U$.

## 10.2.2 Updating The List Of Fired Rules

The *list of fired rules* (*LFR*) is created in order to prevent the inference engine from firing a rule more than once. Thus, if a rule has fired (the certainty of the premise is greater than the given threshold), we add the rule number to the *LFR*.

## 10.2.3 Updating The List Of Fired Concluding Rules

The *list of fired concluding rules* (*LFC*) is created to store those rules that are fired and which contain concluding clauses. A concluding clause is one whose ID (rule plus clause number) is not found in the first two columns of the R-list.

Thus, if a rule is fired, and its conclusion contains concluding clauses, the clause's IDs are placed in the *LFC*. The *LFC* is displayed to the user when the inference process is completed.

### 10.2.4 Searching The R-list

The *relational list* (R-list) is constructed in order to establish the relations between clauses in the conclusion parts of the rules and the clauses in the premise parts of the rules. If a rule is fired, and if the certainty factor and the membership grades are computed for each clause in the conclusion of the fired rule, then the inference process proceeds as follows.

1. Search the *ID* of the fired clause in the first two columns of the R-list. If not found, then we know it is a concluding rule. So at this point the inference engine attempts to fire another rule (see discussion in Chapter 9 on the direct chaining inference process). If the *ID* of the fired conclusion is found in the R-list, then the computation process continues; otherwise, the rule is a concluding rule.

2. Let the clause in the fired conclusion be $c_1$. When the *ID* of $c_1$ is found in the R-list, we extract the *ID* of the linked clause by looking at columns 3 and 4 in the R-list. Let this clause be $c_2$.

3. Go to the rule that contains the clause $c_2$.

4. Update *CF* and *MG* for $c_2$. Let $CF_{c_1}$ and $CF_{c_2}$ be the certainty factors associated with $c_1$ and $c_2$, respectively, and let $MG_{c_1}$ and $MG_{c_2}$ be the membership grades associated with $c_1$ and $c_2$, respectively. Then:

$$CF_{c_2} = \begin{cases} CF_{c_2} \cdot CF_{c_1} & \text{if } CF_{c_2} > 0 \\ CF_{c_1} & \text{otherwise} \end{cases} \qquad (10.24)$$

The membership grade can be computed only if $MG_{c_1}$ is some $\chi_{c_1}$ or $U$, and $MG_{c_2}$ is some $\chi_{c_2}$ or $-1$. Thus:

$$MG_{c_2} = \begin{cases} U & \text{if } MG_{c_1} = U \text{ and } MG_{c_2} = -1 \\ \chi_{c_1} & \text{if } MG_{c_1} = \chi_{c_1} \text{ and } MG_{c_2} = -1 \\ U & \text{if } MG_{c_1} = U \text{ and } MG_{c_2} = \chi_{c_2} \\ min(\chi_{c_1}, \chi_{c_2}) & \text{if } MG_{c_1} = \chi_{c_1} \text{ and } MG_{c_2} = \chi_{c_2} \end{cases} \qquad (10.25)$$

5. Try to fire the rule containing $c_2$. If successful, then repeat the process described in this section, otherwise try the next rule (see Chapter 9).

## 10.3 Example

We conclude this chapter with an example, using the following knowledge base for a control application:

*If the sensor is on Then the water_level is high*

*If the water_level is 60 Then the gate_pressure is high*

Assume that the membership functions defined for the expert system are those given in Table 10.1, and let the *blackboard* have the following data: *sensor is on* with $CF = 0.9$. Also, let the threshold be $T = 0.5$. Then, the inference engine in *FEST* produces the following conclusion:

*The gate_pressure is 94.4 kN high with certainty factor CF = 0.9*

To explain this result, consider Table 10.2 which shows the R-list generated during preprocessing with the given knowledge base. The R-list is interpreted as follows: there is a possible link between the conclusion of rule 1 and the premise of rule 2, resulting in the matching factor of $-1$. If there is indeed such a link, the evaluation of the membership grade, $\chi_{high\_water\_level}(60)$, would result in $MG = 0.78$.

**Table 10.1** Membership functions

| **Fuzzy Variable** | **Range** | **Membership Function** |
|---|---|---|
| *high_gate_pressure* | *[50, 150]* | *S(70, 90, 110)* |
| *high_water_level* | *[40, 80]* | *S(40, 55, 70)* |

**Table 10.2** Generated R-list

| *Conclusion Rule #* | *Conclusion Clause #* | *Premise Rule #* | *Premise Clause #* | *MF* | *MG* |
|---|---|---|---|---|---|
| *1* | *1* | *2* | *1* | *–1* | *0.78* |

Let us turn now to the inferencing process.

- Given the data, the inference engine matches them with the first premise clause in rule 1. Since the premise certainty of *0.9* is greater than the given threshold $T = 0.5$, rule 1 fires with certainty *0.9*.

- Going to the R-list, the inference engine checks that there is a link between the conclusion of rule 1 and the first premise of rule 2 because the subject, *water_level*, is the same in both clauses. Furthermore, the inference engine finds that *high* is a fuzzy variable (it has a membership function associated with it). Hence, the inference engine extracts the preprocessed value $MG = 0.78$ and thus obtains a membership grade of $0.78$ for the premise of rule 2.

Note that the certainty factor of the premise is calculated independently of the membership grade. In this example, the certainty factor for the premise of rule 2 is given by the certainty factor of the conclusion of rule 1, which is $0.9$.

- Finally, the inference engine checks the R-list for the conclusion of rule 2. Since it cannot find the entry, the inference engine concludes that rule 2 is a concluding rule. The inference engine then checks that there is only one concluding clause in rule 2 and finds that it contains a fuzzy variable, *high_gate_pressure*. Hence, using the defuzzification process described in Section 10.2.1, $MG = 0.78$ is applied to the inverse of this function to obtain the domain result of $94.4$.

  Consequently, *FEST* reaches the conclusion that the *gate_pressure* is $94.4$ *kN* high, with a certainty factor of $0.9$.

Assume that we now add the following new rules to our initial knowledge base:

*If the sensor is on Then the water_level is high*

*If the water_level is 60 Then the valve is stuck*

*If the valve is stuck Then the gate_pressure is high*

In this case, the inference engine produces the following conclusion:

*The gate_pressure is high with certainty factor CF = 0.9*

To explain this result, consider Table 10.3 which shows the R-list generated during preprocessing with the given knowledge base. The R-list is interpreted as before as far as the relationship between rule 1 and rule 2 is concerned. With rule 2 and rule 3, it is certain that there is a link between the conclusion of rule 2 and the premise of rule 3, and therefore $MF = 1$. Since the *valve is stuck* is a regular sentence, it is certain that it cannot influence the membership grade of *gate_pressure is high*, hence, $MG = -2$.

**Table 10.3** Generated R-list

| Conclusion Rule # | Conclusion Clause # | Premise Rule # | Premise Clause # | MF | MG |
|---|---|---|---|---|---|
| 1 | 1 | 2 | 1 | −1 | 0.78 |
| 2 | 1 | 3 | 1 | 1 | −2 |

What about the inferencing process?

- Up to the premise of rule 2, the evaluation is the same as before.
- At the conclusion of rule 2, the inference engine detects from the R-list that there is a direct match between the conclusion of rule 2 and the premise of rule 3. Since the question of membership is being resolved here, and since the membership grade obtained from the premise of rule 2 resets to −2, the certainty factor simply carries over to rule 3.
- On reaching the conclusion of rule 3, the inference engine detects that there is a fuzzy variable. However, since there is no membership grade defined for this variable, the membership evaluation is ignored. Consequently, the final conclusion is that of a regular clause, *the gate_pressure is high* with certainty factor $CF = 0.9$.

# 11 FUZZY INFERENCING IN FEST

In this chapter we describe how *FEST* implements the fuzzy inferencing procedure described in Chapter 10. When we choose the *ES-Shell* option from *FEST*'s main menu, we obtain the sub-menu shown in Figure 2.4 of Chapter 2 which consists of six options.

1. *Input data.* Allows the user place to data onto the blackboard.

2. *Infer.* Invokes the fuzzy inference engine to run the inference procedures.

3. *Display blackboard.* Allows the user to observe the blackboard.

4. *Display conclusions.* Displays the concluding rules. Note that this is valid only if an inference has been done.

5. *Explain.* Allows the user to view the reasoning path. Note that this is valid only if an inference has been done.

6. *Clear Blackboard.* Clears and re-initializes the blackboard.

We discuss these options in detail in the following sections.

## 11.1 Input Data

This option allows the user to input the data and stores them on the blackboard. Each data item is in a proposition form and has to be inserted one proposition per line. There are two ways to load data onto the blackboard.

1.   *Non-interactive mode.* As described in Chapter 2, we can load the data from a
     data file by invoking *FEST* in the following way:

                                    *FEST KB DATA*

     If we choose this option from the DOS environment, *FEST* is loaded first and,
     then, it loads the knowledge base *KB* (as described in Chapter 8), and loads
     the data file *DATA* onto the blackboard.
         Propositions are stored in the blackboard as plain ASCII text using the
     following format:

                                *P, Certainty Factor (CF)*

     where *P* designates the proposition and the certainty factor *CF* assumes a
     value between *0* to *1*.

2.   *Interactive mode.* When we choose *Input Data, FEST*'s editor is invoked. The
     editor accepts one proposition at a time, parses it, and validates it. If the
     proposition is legal, *FEST* loads it onto the blackboard, as shown in Figure
     11.1.

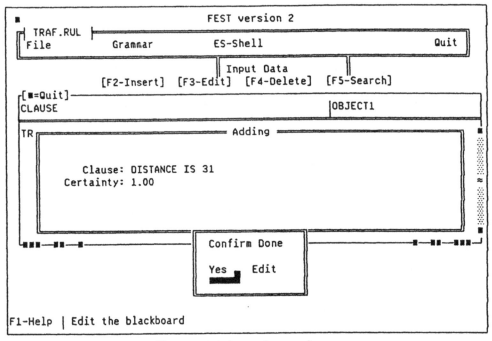

**Figure 11.1** Input data option

One major difference between the interactive and the non-interactive modes is evident
when we want to enter a proposition that contains the keyword *not*. *FEST* treats this
case in the following way.

1. In the *interactive mode*, *FEST* pauses and asks us to provide the domain limits for a particular variable.

2. In the *non-interactive mode*, we have to provide *FEST* with the proposition and the possible range of the domains as well as the certainty factor (CF). Consider the proposition *P* and let the range for the domain be [*α, β*]. Then, the data are entered as follows:

$$P; \alpha, \beta, CF$$

where the certainty factor is a number between *0* and *1*.

Following the parsing of the data and placing all the necessary pieces in their proper places, the inference process can take place.

## 11.2 Infer

The inference process is based on the inferencing procedure described in Chapter 10. When we choose the *Infer* option, *FEST* opens a window and displays the inference process. In other words, *FEST* displays information regarding the current event during every step of the inference process. As shown in Figure 11.2, this information includes the number of the rule being processed, any membership function(s) being evaluated, any mathematical expression(s) being evaluated, etc.

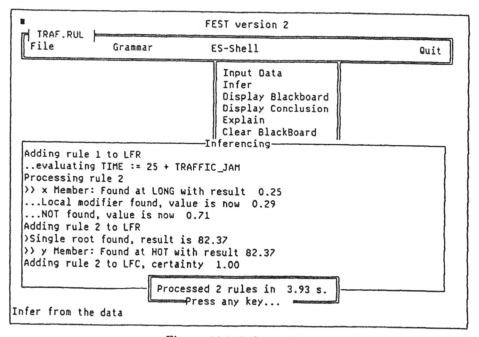

**Figure 11.2** Infer option

After completing the inference process, *FEST* displays information regarding the time it took to perform the inferencing procedure. If the items displayed are more than can be contained on one screen, *FEST* automatically invokes a browser window which allows us to scroll back and view the inference process that had just taken place. Note that in the *non-interactive mode*, we see only the inference process being displayed, without any pauses.

The displays are provided to reassure us that an inference procedure is indeed taking place, and to allow us to observe the sequence of events. To return to the main menu, press the **ESC** key to transfer control to the *ES-Shell* main menu item.

Now that the inference process has been completed, we can choose to examine the results, inspect the blackboard contents, or query *FEST* about the reasoning path.

## 11.3  Display Blackboard

The blackboard contains all the information provided by the user (in the *interactive mode*) or by some data file (in the *non-interactive mode*). Each entry in the blackboard is a parsed version of a proposition and it is displayed as a premise file (see Chapter 8).

The blackboard also contains some intermediate results that are caused by the evaluation of a mathematical expression and by the evaluation of a membership function. Note that intermediate conclusions are not placed on the blackboard. Since all the information is embedded in the clauses themselves, there is no need to place this information on the blackboard.

The *Display Blackboard* option stems from the knowledge validation process. If we want to inspect the results of the inference process, we can view the blackboard to see if the data stored there are consistent with what we expect to see.

## 11.4  Display Conclusions

After completing the inference process, all the concluding rules are placed in the *list of fired concluding rules* (*LFC*) and listed in a descending order. If the inference engine produces more than one conclusion, the first conclusion on the *LFC* will have the highest certainty factor whereas the last conclusion will have the lowest certainty factor.

There are two way to display the conclusions.

1.  In the *interactive mode*, we choose the *Display Conclusion* option and *FEST* displays all the conclusions and their associated certainty factors.

2.  In the *non-interactive mode*, *FEST* transforms the contents of the *LFC* into a specified file. Thus, if we invoke *FEST* using the command line:

*FEST  KB DATA OUTFILE*

(see Chapter 2), *FEST* loads the specified knowledge base (*KB*) into the proper data structures, the data (*DATA*) onto the blackboard, and then performs the inference process. Upon completing the inference process, the results are transferred into the output file (*OUTFILE*).

When the conclusion is associated with a membership function, the clause is displayed together with the associated value that is extracted from the membership function, as shown in Figure 11.3.

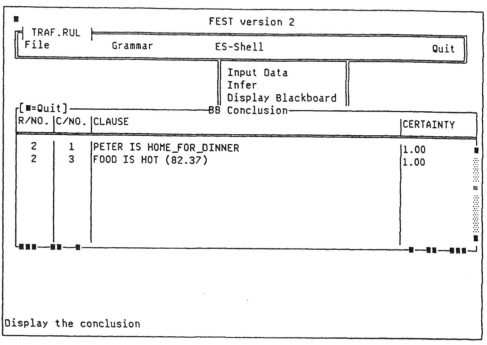

**Figure 11.3** Displaying conclusions

## 11.5 Explain

The explanation program is designed to let us view and inspect the reasoning path derived from the inference procedure. Choosing the *Explain* option invokes the explain screen where we are requested to provide a rule number. The rule number serves as a leaf node for the backward tracing of the inference process, as shown in Figure 11.4.

Having provided the rule number, say *N*, the explanation procedure first checks if the rule associated with *N* has fired, that is, that the rule is in the *list of fired rules* (*LFR*). If it is found, then the backtracking process takes place.

1.   Search for rule *N* in the third column in the R-list.

2.    If rule $N$ is not found, then the firing of the rule stems from the user-provided data.

3.    If rule $N$ is found, then assign the value of the first column in the R-list to rule $M$.

4.    Print rule $M$.

5.    Ask the user for the next rule number.

Thus, each time we provide a rule number $N$ to the explanation facility in *FEST*, the explanation procedure explains why this rule has fired. This process continues until the **ESC** key is pressed.

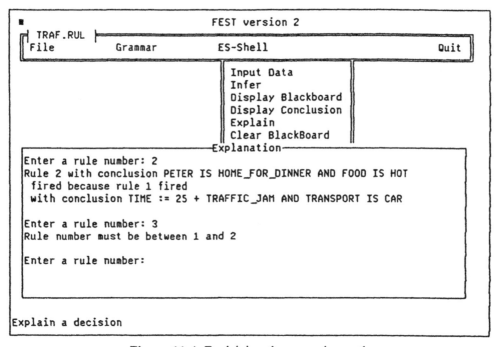

**Figure 11.4** Explaining the reasoning path

The explanation procedure is a very important feature in the design of expert systems for several reasons.

1.    For expert system designers, it is important because they can check sample knowledge bases and validate that the expert system does what it is supposed to do.

2.    For knowledge engineers, it is important because they can check if the knowledge is complete and properly validated.

3. For end users, it is important because they can relate to the inference process of the expert system and verify that the expert system does what it is supposed to do.

## 11.6  Clear Blackboard

The *Clear Blackboard* option allows us to clear the blackboard and to remove any existing data from it. Usually, this feature is used when we want to perform another inference procedure using a new set of data. In other words, it allows us to reuse the blackboard for different data sets.

# REFERENCES

[1] Adlassnig, K. P., and G. Kolarz (1986), "Representation and Semiautomatic Acquisition of Medical Knowledge in Cardiac-1 and Cardiac-2", *Computers and Biomedical Research*, Vol. 19, pp. 63 - 79.

[2] Baldwin, J. F. (1985), "Fuzzy Sets and Expert Systems", *Information Sciences*, Vol. 36, pp. 123 - 156.

[3] Barr, A. and E. A. Feigenbaum (1981), *The Handbook of Artificial Intelligence*, Vol. I, William Kaufmann.

[4] Bellman, R. E. and L. A. Zadeh (1970), "Decision-Making in a Fuzzy Environment", *Management Science*, No.17, pp. 141 - 164.

[5] Ben-Bassat, M. *et al.* (1988), "AITEST - A Real Life Expert System for Electronic Troubleshooting", *Proc. 4th Conference on AI Applications*, IEEE Computer Society Press.

[6] Bibel, W. (1983), "Knowledge Representation From a Deductive Point of View", *Proc. IFAC Symposium*, V. M. Ponomaryov (ed.), Leningrad, USSR, Oct. 1983, Pergamon Press.

[7] Black, M. (1970), *Margins of Precision: Essays in Logic and Language*, Cornell University Press.

[8] Bonnet, A., J. P. Haton, and J. M. Truong-Ngoc (1988), *Expert Systems*, Prentice-Hall.

[9] Buckley, J. J., W. Siler, and D. Tucker (1986), "A Fuzzy Expert System", *Fuzzy Sets and Systems*, Vol. 20, pp. 1 - 16.

[10] Chaplin, J. P. (1985), *Dictionary of Psychology*, 2nd Edition, Dell Publishing.

[11] Chen, K., and S. C. Lu (1988), "A Machine Learning Approach to Automatic Synthesis of Mechanistic Knowledge for Engineering Decision-Making", *Proc. 4th Conference on AI Applications*, IEEE Computer Society Press.

[12] Codd, E. F. (1970), "A Relational Model of Data for Large Shared Data Banks", *Communications of ACM*, Vol. 13, pp. 377 - 387.

[13] Codd, E. F. (1979), "Extending the Database Relational Model to Capture More Meaning", *ACM Trans. on Database Systems*, Vol. 4, pp. 397 - 434.

[14] Codd, E. F. (1971), "Further Normalization of the Database Relational Model", in *Database Systems*, R. Rustin (ed.), Courant Computer Science Symposia 6, Prentice-Hall, pp. 65 - 98.

[15] Date, C. J. (1981), *An Introduction to Database Systems*, 3rd Edition, Addison-Wesley.

[16] Dempster, A. P. (1967), "Upper and Lower Probabilities Induced by Multivalued Mappings", *Annals of Mathematical Statistics*, Vol. 39, pp. 325 - 329.

[17] Dubois, D., and H. Prade (1980), *Fuzzy Sets and Systems: Theory and Applications*, Academic Press.

[18] Duda, R. O. *et al.* (1978), *Development of the Prospector Consultation System For Mineral Exploration*, SRI International Technical Report.

[19] Duda, R., H. Gaschnig, and P. Hart (1979), "Model Design in the PROSPECTOR Consultant System for Mineral Exploration", in *Expert Systems in the Micro-Electronic Age*, D. Michie (ed.), Edinburgh University Press.

[20] Erman, L. D., and V. R. Lesser (1983), "The Hearsay II Speech Understanding System: A Tutorial", *Proc. IFAC Symposium*, V. M. Ponomaryov (ed.), Leningrad, USSR.

[21] Enrick, N. L. (1978), *Industrial Engineering Manual for the Textile Industry*, Krieger Publishing Co.

[22] Feigenbaum, E., G. Buchnan, and J. Lederberg (1971), "Generality and Problem Solving: A Case Study Using the DENDRAL Program", *Machine Intelligence*, Vol. 6., pp. 165 - 190.

[23] Fieschi, M. *et al.* (1982), "SPINX - A System for Computer Aided Diagnosis", *Methods of Information in Medicine*, Vol. 21, pp. 143 - 148.

[24] Fischer, C., and R. LeBlanc (1988), *Crafting a Compiler*, Benjamin/Cummings.

[25] Friedman, M., M. Schneider, and A. Kandel (1989), "The Use of Weighted Fuzzy Expected Value (WFEV) in Fuzzy Expert Systems", *Fuzzy Sets and Systems*, Vol. 31, pp.37 - 45.

[26] Gaines, B. R., and M. Shaw (1985), "From Fuzzy Logic to Expert systems", *Information Sciences*, Vol. 36, pp. 5 - 16.

[27] Gazdar, G., and C. Mellish (1989), *Natural Language Processing in Prolog - An Introduction to Computational Statistics*, Addison-Wesley.

[28] Giarratano, J., and G. Riley (1989), *Expert Systems - Principles and Programming*, PWS-KENT Publishing Co.

[29] Goguen, J. A. (1975), "On Fuzzy Robot Planning", in *Fuzzy Sets and Their Applications to Cognitive and Decision Processes*, Academic Press, pp. 429 - 448.

[30] Good, D., and R. London (1970), "Computer Interval Arithmetic: Definition and Proof of Correct Implementation", *Journal of the ACM*, Vol. 4, pp. 603 - 612.

[31] Grady, P. L., and G. N. Mock (1990), "Electronics in Textiles 1990", *Proc. Electronics in Textiles Conference*, Clemson, South Carolina, March 28 - 29.

[32] Grant, J. (1977), "Null Values in a Relational Database", *Information Processing Letters*, Vol. 6, pp. 156 - 157.

[33] Grzymala-Busse (1991), *Managing Uncertainty in Expert Systems*, Kluwer Academic Publishers.

[34] Gupta, M. M., and T. Yamakawa (1988), *Fuzzy Logic in Knowledge-Based Systems*, North-Holland.

[35] Gupta, M. M., A. Kandel, W. Bandler, and J. B. Kizka (1985), *Approximate Reasoning in Expert Systems*, North-Holland.

[36] Harmon, P., and D. King (1985), *Expert Systems*, John Wiley & Sons.

[37] Harris, M. (1985), *Introduction to Natural Language Processing*, Reston Publishing Company, pp. 227 - 238.

[38] Hart, J. (1990), "The Computer Integrated Textile Enterprise", *Proc. Electronics in Textiles Conference*, Clemson, South Carolina, March 28 - 29.

[39] Hayes-Roth, F., D. A. Waterman, and D. B. Lenat (1983), *Building Expert Systems*, Addison-Wesley.

[40] Jackson, P. (1990), *Introduction to Expert Systems*, Addison-Wesley.

[41] Jones, P. (1986), "REVEAL - Approximate Reasoning", in *A Fuzzy Expert System*, J. J. Buckley *et al* (eds.), *Fuzzy Sets and Systems*, Vol. 20, pp. 1 - 16.

[42] Joseph, L. M. (1984), *Essentials of Textiles*, Holt, Rinehart and Winston.

[43] Joshi, R., and M. Schneider (1990), "Knowledge Representation in Fuzzy Relational Databases", *Proc. FLAIRS-90*, Cocoa Beach, Florida, April 3 - 6, pp. 122 - 126.

[44] Kandel, A. (1982), *Fuzzy Techniques in Pattern Recognition*, John Wiley & Sons.

[45] Kandel, A. (1986), *Fuzzy Mathematical Techniques with Applications*, Addison-Wesley.

[46] Kandel, A. (1991), *Fuzzy Expert Systems*, CRC Press.

[47] Kandel, A., and G. Langholz (1992), *Hybrid Architectures for Intelligent Systems*, CRC Press.

[48] Kandel, A., M. Schneider, and G. Langholz (1992), "The Use of Fuzzy Logic For the Management of Uncertainty in Intelligent Hybrid Systems", in *Fuzzy Logic for the Management of Uncertainty*, L. A. Zadeh and J. Kacprzyk (eds.), John Wiley & Sons.

[49] Kaufmann, A., and M. M. Gupta (1985), *Introduction to Fuzzy Arithmetic: Theory and Applications*, Van Nostrand Rheinhold.

[50] Kaufmann, A. (1975), *An Introduction to the Theory of Fuzzy Subsets*, Vol. 1, Academic Press.

[51] Klir, J. G. (1987), "Where Do We Stand on Measures of Uncertainty, Ambiguity, Fuzziness, and the Like?", *Fuzzy Sets and Systems*, Vol. 24, pp. 141 - 161.

[52] Kowalski, R. (1987), *Logic for Problem Solving*, Elsevier North Holland.

[53] Kulikowski, C. (1980), "Artificial Intelligence Methods and Systems for Medical Consultation", *IEEE Trans. on Pattern Analysis and Machine Intelligence*, Vol. 2, pp. 464 - 476.

[54] Labov, W. (1973), "The Boundaries of Words and their Meanings", in *New Ways of Analyzing Variation in English*, N. Baily and R. W. Shuy (eds.), Georgetown University Press.

[55] Lakoff, G. (1973), "A Study in Meaning Criteria and the Logic of Fuzzy Concepts", *Journal of Philosophy*, No. 2, pp. 458 - 508.

[56] Liebowitz, J. (1988), *Introduction to Expert Systems*, Mitchell Publishing.

[57] Lipski, W. Jr. (1979), "On Semantic Issues Connected with Incomplete Information Databases", *ACM Trans. on Database Systems*, Vol. 4, pp. 262 - 296.

[58] Luger, G. F., and W. A. Stubblefield (1989), *Artificial Intelligence and the Design of Expert Systems*, Benjamin/Cummings.

[59] Lafaivre, R. (1974), *Fuzzy: A Programming Language for Fuzzy Problem-Solving*, Technical Report 202, Computer Sciences Department, University of Wisconsin, Madison.

[60] Matin, J., and S. W. Oxman (1988), *Building Expert Systems*, Prentice-Hall.

[61] Maier, D. (1983), *The Theory of Relational Databases*, CRC Press.

[62] McGraw, K. L., and K. Harbison-Briggs (1989), *Knowledge Acquisition - Principles and Guidelines*, Prentice-Hall.

[63] Minsky, M. (1967), *Computation: Finite and Infinite Machines*, Prentice-Hall.

[64] Mizumoto, M., S. Fukami, and K. Tanaka (1979), "Some Methods of Fuzzy Reasoning", in *Advances in Fuzzy Set Theory and Applications*, M. M. Gupta, R. K. Ragade, and R. R. Yager (eds.), North-Holland, pp. 117 - 136.

[65] Mizumoto, M., and K. Tanaka (1976), "Some Properties of Fuzzy Sets of Type 2", *Information and Control*, Vol. 31, pp. 312 - 340.

[66] Moore, R. (1975), *Mathematical Elements of Scientific Computing*, Holt, Rinehart and Winston.

[67] Moore, R. (1979), *Methods and Applications of Interval Analysis*, SIAM, Philadelphia, PA.

[68] Mosier, C. I. (1941), "A Psychometric Study of Meaning", *Journal of Social Psychology*, No.13, pp. 123 - 140.

[69] Nakamura, H. *et al* (1988), "Life Term Prediction of Hydro Power Steel Structures Based on Knowledge Engineering Techniques", *Proc. 4th Conference on AI Applications*, IEEE Computer Society Press, Washington, DC.

[70] Nahmias, S. (1978), "Fuzzy Variables", *Fuzzy Sets and Systems*, Vol. 1, pp. 97 - 100.

[71] Negoita, C. V. (1985), *Expert Systems and Fuzzy Systems*, Benjamin/Cummings.

[72] Orlov, A. I. (1980), *Problems of Optimization and Fuzzy Variables*, Znaniye, Moscow.

[73] Prade H. (1980), "Fuzzy Programming: Why and How? - Some Hints and Examples", *Proc. 4th IEEE International Conference on Computer Software and Applications*, pp. 237 - 251.

[74] Pereir, L. M., and E. Oliviera (1984), "Prolog For Expert Systems: A Case Study", *Proc. IFAC Symposium*, V. M. Ponomaryov (ed.), Leningrad, USSR, Oct. 1984, Pergamon Press.

[75] Ralescu, D. *et al.* (1987), *Simulation, Knowledge-Based Computing and Fuzzy Statistics*, Van Nostrand Reinhold.

[76] Reiter, R. (1984), "On Closed World Databases", in *Logic and Databases*, H. Gallaire and J. Minker (eds.), Plenum Press, pp. 191 - 233.

[77] Rich, E. (1983), *Artificial Intelligence*, McGraw-Hill, pp. 180 - 183.

[78] Richards, T. (1989), *Clausal Form Logic - An Introduction to Logic of Computer Reasoning*, Addison-Wesley.

[79] Ruspini, E. H. (1982), "Possibility Theory Approaches for Advanced Information Systems", *IEEE Computer*, Vol. 9, pp. 83 - 89.

[80] Saaty, T. L. (1980), *The Analytic Hierarchy Process - Planning Priority Setting, Resource Allocation*, McGraw-Hill.

[81] Schneider, M., and A. Kandel (1988), *Cooperative Fuzzy Expert Systems - Their Design and Applications in Intelligent Recognition*, Verlag TUV, Rheinland.

[82] Schneider, M., and A. Kandel (1988), "Properties of the Fuzzy Expected Value and the Fuzzy Expected Interval", *Fuzzy Sets and Systems*, Vol. 26, pp. 373 - 385.

[83] Schneider, M., and A. Kandel (1988), "Properties of the Fuzzy Expected Value and the Fuzzy Expected Interval in Fuzzy Environment", *Fuzzy Sets and Systems*, Vol. 28, pp. 55 - 68.

[84] Schneider, M., E. Shnaider, and A. Kandel (1990), "Application of the Negation Operator in Fuzzy Production Rules", *Fuzzy Sets and Systems*, Vol. 34, pp. 293 - 299.

[85] Schneider, M., D. Clark, and A. Kandel (1990), "The Matching Process in Fuzzy Expert Systems", *Proc. 3rd International IPMU Conference*, Paris, France, July 2 - 6.

[86] Schneider, M. and A. Kandel (1992), "On Uncertainty Management in Fuzzy Inference Procedures", *Proc. 1st International Conference on Fuzzy Theory and Technology, Control and Decision*, Durham, North Carolina.

[87] Shah, R. P. (1988), "JET-X: Jet Engine Troubleshooting Expert System", *Proc. International Workshop on Artificial Intelligence for Industrial Applications*, IEEE Publishing Services.

[88] Shortliffe, E. H. (1976), *Computer-Based Medical Consultation: MYCIN*, Elsevier North Holland.

[89] Siler, W., J. Buckley, and D. Tucker (1987), "Functional Requirements for a Fuzzy Expert System Shell", in *Approximate Reasoning in Intelligent Systems, Decision and Control*, E. Sanchez and L. A. Zadeh. (eds.), Pergamon Press, pp. 21 - 31.

[90] Smith, C. B., and J. W. Rucker (1987), "Troubleshooting in Preparation - A Systematic Approach", *American Dyestuff Reporter*, Vol. 76:9, pp. 34 - 57.

[91] Smith, M. H. *et al.* (1975), "The Design of Jason - A Computer Controlled Mobile Robot", *Proc. IEEE System, Man and Cybernetics Conference*, San Francisco.

[92] Stefik, M. *et al.* (1982), "The Organization of Expert Systems - A Tutorial", *Artificial Intelligence*, Vol. 18, pp. 135 - 173.

[93] Sterling, L., and E. Shapiro (1986), *The Art of Prolog*, MIT Press.

[94] Talbot, C. J. (1988), "Scheduling TV Advertising: An Expert Systems Approach to Utilizing Fuzzy Knowledge", *Proc. 4th Australian Conference Application in Expert Systems*, Sydney, Australia.

[95] Tanaka, T., and N. Sueda (1988), "Knowledge Acquisition in Image Processing - Expert System EXPLAIN", *Proc. International Workshop on AI for Industrial Applications*, IEEE Publishing.

[96] Tanimoto, S. L. (1987), *The Elements of AI*, IEEE Computer Science Press, pp. 89 - 91.

[97] Vassiliou, Y. (1979), "Null Values in Relational Management: A Denotational Semantics Approach", *Proc. ACM SIGMOD International Conference on Management of Data*, Boston, pp. 260 - 269.

[98] Wagman, D., M. Schneider, and E. Shnaider (1993), "On the Use of Interval Mathematics in Fuzzy Expert Systems", *International Journal of Intelligent Systems*.

[99] Waterman, D. A. (1985), *A Guide to Expert Systems*, Addison-Wesley.

[100] Wechsler, H. (1976), "Fuzzy Approach to Medical Diagnosis", *International Journal of Biomedical Computing*, Vol. 7, pp.191 - 203.

[101] Weiss, S. M., and C. A. Kulikowski (1984), *Designing Expert Systems*, Rowman and Allanheld.

[102] Weiskamp, K., and T. Hengl (1988), *AI Programming with Turbo Prolog*, John Wiley & Sons.

[103] Wheeler, M., and M. Schneider (1990), "Automatic Knowledge Acquisition for Expert Systems", *Proc. Symposium on Applied Computing*, Fayetteville, Arkansas, April 5 - 6, pp. 96 - 101.

[104] Wheeler, M., and M. Schneider (1991), "Input Validation For AUTOKNAQ: Knowledge Acquisition System", *Proc. International Conference on Systems, Man and Cybernetics*, Charlottesville, Virginia, October 13 - 16.

[105] Wheeler, M., and M. Schneider (1992), "AUTOKNAQ: Automatic Knowledge Acquisition for Fault Isolation Expert Systems", *Proc. Symposium on Applied Computing*, Kansas City, Kansas, March 1 - 3, pp. 387 - 395.

[106] Winston, P. (1984), *Artificial Intelligence*, Addison-Wesley.

[107] Zadeh, L. A. (1976), "Outline of a New Approach to the Analysis of Complex Systems and Decision Processes", *IEEE Transactions on Systems, Man and Cybernetics*, Vol.3, pp. 28 - 44

[108] Zadeh, L. A. (1962), "From Circuit Theory to System Theory", *Proc. Institute of Radio Engineers*, Vol. 50, pp. 856 - 865.

[109] Zadeh, L. A. (1965), "Fuzzy Sets", *Information and Control*, Vol. 8, pp. 338 - 353.

[110] Zadeh, L. A. (1970), "Decision Making in a Fuzzy Environment", *Management Science*, Vol. 17, pp. 141 - 164.

[111] Zadeh, L. A. (1973), "Outline of a New Approach to the Analysis of Complex Systems and Decision Processes", *IEEE Transactions on Systems, Man, and Cybernetics*, Vol. 3, pp. 28 - 44.

[112] Zadeh, L. A. (1975), "The Concept of a Linguistic Variable and its Application to Approximate Reasoning", Part I, *Information Sciences*, Vol. 8, pp. 199 - 249; Part II, *Information Sciences*, Vol. 8, pp. 301 - 357; Part III, *Information Sciences*, Vol. 9, pp. 43 - 80.

[113] Zadeh, L. A. (1975), *Calculus of Fuzzy Restrictions In Fuzzy Sets and Their Applications to Cognitive and Decision Processes*. Academic Press.

[114] Zadeh, L. A. (1977), "Theory of Fuzzy Reasoning and Probability Theory vs. Possibility Theory in Decision Making", *Proc. Symposium on Fuzzy Set Theory and Applications*, IEEE Conf. on Decision and Control, New Orleans.

[115] Zadeh, L. A. (1978), "Fuzzy Sets as Basis for Theory of Possibility", *Fuzzy Sets and Systems*, Vol. 1, pp. 3 - 28.

[116] Zadeh, L. A. (1983), "The Role of Fuzzy Logic in the Management of Uncertainty in Expert systems", *Fuzzy Sets and Systems*, Vol. 11, pp. 199 - 227.

[117] Zadeh, L. A. (1983), *Commonsense Knowledge representation Based on Fuzzy Logic*, ERL Memo M83/26, University of California, Berkeley.

[118] Zadeh, L. A. (1983), "A Computational Approach to Fuzzy Quantifiers in Natural Languages", *Comp. and Math. with Applications.* pp. 149 - 184.

[119] Zamankova-Leech, M. and A. Kandel (1984), *Fuzzy Relational Databases - A Key to Expert Systems*, Verlag TUV, Rheinland.

[120] Zejnilovic, A., and M. Schneider (1990), "The Role of Fuzzy Expert Systems in the Textile Industry", *Proc. Electronics in Textiles Conference*, March 27 - 28, Clemson, South Carolina.

[121] Zimmermann, H. J. (1987), *Fuzzy Set Theory and Its Applications*, Nijhoff.

[122] Zimmermann, H. J. (1978), "Fuzzy Programming and Linear Programming with Several Objective Functions", *Fuzzy Sets and Systems*, Vol. 1, pp. 45 - 55.

# INDEX

Printed and bound by CPI Group (UK) Ltd, Croydon, CR0 4YY

27/10/2024

14580216-0001